CONCILIUM

Religion in the Eighties

CONCILIUM

Concilium 148 (8/1981): Ecumenism

WHO HAS THE SAY IN THE CHURCH?

Edited by
Jürgen Moltmann
and
Hans Küng

English Language Editor
Marcus Lefébure

T. & T. CLARK LTD.
Edinburgh

THE SEABURY PRESS
New York

October 1981
T. & T. Clark Ltd., 36 George Street, Edinburgh EH2 2LQ
ISBN: 0 567 30028 5

The Seabury Press, 815 Second Avenue, New York, N.Y. 10017
ISBN: 0 8164 2348 2

Library of Congress Catalog Card No.: 80 54390

Printed in Scotland by William Blackwood & Sons Ltd., Edinburgh

Concilium: Monthly except July and August.
Subscriptions 1981: All countries (except U.S.A. and Canada) £27·00 postage and handling included; U.S.A. and Canada $64.00 postage and handling included. (Second class postage licence 541-530 at New York, N.Y.) Subscription distribution in U.S. by Expediters of the Printed Word Ltd., 527 Madison Avenue, Suite 1217, New York, N.Y. 10022.

CONTENTS

Foreword: Who has the say in the Church?

Dear readers of *Concilium*,

As a result of the most recent disputes within the Catholic Church the executive committee of the international review of theology *Concilium* has decided to change the subject-matter of the 1981 issue on ecumenism at short notice and to devote it to the question of the *magisterium* and theology.

But, you may perhaps ask, is not the question of the *magisterium* a typically Catholic problem?

Yes, to the extent that this question arises with particular sharpness in the centralistic Roman system with its powerful 'authentic *magisterium*'.

No, to the extent that the question of teaching authority arises in every church, including the Protestant and Orthodox churches, and that it divides many churches from each other.

Hence the specifically Roman as well as the ecumenical aspects of the problem need to be considered under a heading that brings out both its fundamental and its critical quality—the question: 'Who has the say in the Church?'

In tackling this problem certain presuppositions are taken for granted both by the contributors to and by the editors of this issue. They are presuppositions that surely apply to all Christian churches.

Because the Church is the Church of God, his people and his possession, God himself has the say, the decisive word, in the Church.

But because this Church of God is at the same time the Church of Jesus Christ, the community of his disciples and his body, Jesus Christ is in the Church the visible word of the invisible God, the word made flesh that for the Church is the actual way the critical truth and the true life.

And because finally the Church of God and Jesus Christ is the Church of the Spirit, his living spiritual temple, it is the Holy Spirit of God and Jesus Christ that continually leads the Church into the truth and maintains it in the truth.

On the basis of these common Christian presuppositions our contributors from the different churches have concentrated on the actual question: How is what God has to say to the Church through Jesus Christ in the Holy Spirit passed on correctly? In what way is the gospel of Jesus Christ borne witness to in the Church and world of today in a manner that does justice both to the contents of the message and the times we are living in? What are the structures by means of which the Church is maintained in the truth by the Holy Spirit—the Church that has a horizontal dimension alongside the vertical one and consists of human beings who sin and go astray?

In answering this question our contributors have been able to rely on the existence of the report on the consultation held in Odessa in 1978 by the Faith and Order

Commission of the World Council of Churches. This report is very illuminating on the divergences and convergences that occur with regard to binding doctrine in the Church. The Commission's general secretary at the time, Lukas Vischer, has been good enough to abridge this report to a compass that is within the bounds of this journal. At the same time the Catholic exegete Bas van Iersel has sought to answer the question: Who according to the New Testament has or should have the say in the Church? In this he brings out clearly how in the New Testament, apart from the pastoral epistles, it is not the individual officials but the assembled community that has the decisive word to say in matters of doctrine and morals. This raises the question how we are to judge the later development of the Church, a development that is above all based on the pastoral epistles. The theological positions taken up in the next contribution may help in forming such a judgment.

How does the Church today remain in the truth? The different contributors tackling this question represent the most important positions adopted by the various churches today, and each should be fully representative of his particular church. Their contributions are well-rounded and to the point, critical and self-critical, in a word ecumenical in the best sense of that term. Boris Bobrinskoy (Paris) provides an Orthodox answer, Ulrich Kühn (Leipzig) a Lutheran one and Harry M. Kuitert (Amstelveen) a Reformed answer. The Anglican answer comes from Stephen W. Sykes (Durham), that of the Free Churches from Olle Engström (Lidingö), and the Old Catholic answer—particularly important in the present context—from Kurt Stalder (Berne).

The Catholic position, which is above all what is at issue here, is tackled from various sides. The first thing to be done is to clarify some problematical concepts that continually create fresh confusion both within the Catholic Church and among Christians generally. Leonardo Boff (Petrópolis) deals with the question: Is the distinction between the *ecclesia docens* and the *ecclesia discens* justified? Gabriel Daly (Dublin) tackles the question: Which *magisterium* is 'authentic'? Luigi Sartori (Padua) tries to answer the question: What is the criterion for the *sensus fidelium*?

Since so much is made by official and semi-official theology of the apostolic succession of the Church's ministries of leadership, we thought it apposite to take up once again the subject of the succession of prophets and teachers in the Church, a subject that for the most part seems to have fallen into oblivion. This is done by Avery Dulles (Washington, D.C.) under the title: *Successio apostolorum—successio prophetarum—successio doctorum*. Finally we have called on the grand old man of the renewal of Catholic ecclesiology, Yves Congar (Paris), to attempt a Catholic synthesis. Congar puts forward an ecumenically open Catholic position that could certainly be subscribed to by the majority of Catholic theologians today. The question of infallibility that Congar only touches on marginally is dealt with in the Bulletin, where the Catholic Church historian Georg Denzler (Bamberg) reports on the course of the debate on infallibility in Germany, a debate which has been given fresh critical emphasis by the publications on Vatican I of the Catholic historian Bernhard Hasler, whose premature death we regret.

Anyone who studies this volume from cover to cover will easily be able to establish examples of convergence and divergence. Here we should merely like to draw attention to a few points that strike us as particularly important.

(1) Who has the say in the Church? Yves Congar has provided the fundamental answer, one that ought to be accepted by all the churches, when he talks of 'one single Church which as a whole listens, celebrates, loves, confesses, and in which everyone is challenged to exercise his or her function. It is the whole Church that learns, it is the whole Church that teaches, but in different ways. The Fathers testify to this verity in abundance.'

(2) What is the norm for what is said in the Church? For everything that men and women say the norm is the Word of God, the gospel of Jesus Christ, the witness of the Holy Spirit, as this was originally deposited in the holy scriptures of the Old and New Covenant. Subordinate to this are the various traditions that are given different valuations in the different churches. It is on the basis of scripture and following the line of its tradition that each church speaks through its liturgy (whether universal or local) and through its institutions (which can of course disavow what they say by what they do).

(3) To what extent is it necessary to differentiate between human statements? What remains fundamental is that according to the function in the Church that belongs to him or her every Christian has something to say and that this freedom of a Christian man or woman may not be suppressed by any authority whatsoever or reduced to something purely marginal. The voice of the individual and even more the voice of the various communities should be heard with attention whenever it expresses the Word of God, the gospel, the witness of the Spirit. In all churches, however, a special status is accorded *de iure* or *de facto* to the pastoral ministries of leadership (parish priests, bishops) and in another manner to theologians, to prophetic figures, to holy men and women.

It is at this point that disagreement arises. What doctrinal authority is possessed by bishops, parish priests, theologians, charismatic individuals, the 'ordinary' Christians? The range of answers, from the Roman position to that of the Free Churches, covers the entire spectrum, and it would be advisable, bearing in mind every church's problematical past as well as the better ecumenical future that is hoped for, to examine carefully the strengths and the weaknesses of the positions of every church. In this process every church will be able to draw both theoretical and practical lessons from all the others, and agreement in essentials is surely not excluded for the future, given honest reflection on the original Christian witness.

What emerges from all the non-Catholic contributions as well as from the Bulletin on the debate among Catholics is that only one question would seem to remain the great stumbling-block on the road to ecumenical agreement, a stumbling-block that only Rome can move: the question of papal infallibility. Many contributions point to the importance of dialogue. Ought not a dialogue in a Christian spirit to be possible with Rome on this question too?   .

Yours ecumenically,

Jürgen Moltmann.
Hans Küng.

Translated by Robert Nowell

Lukas Vischer

I. How does the church teach authoritatively today?

In 1974, the Faith and Order Commission of the World Council of Churches initiated a study on this theme. On the basis of a working paper groups in several countries (Italy, Federal Republic of Germany, German Democratic Republic, Greece) considered particular aspects. In 1977 an international ecumenical consultation involving representatives from different confessional traditions took place in Odessa, USSR. The following paper is a shortened version of the report issued by this meeting.

Lukas Vischer

The ultimate concern of this study is the faithful witness of the Church today to the gospel of Jesus Christ as it was proclaimed by the apostles and the apostolic Church. The Church, called into being and kept alive through the centuries by the Spirit, has the responsibility to make known the apostolic truth both to its own members and to the world. How does it fulfil this task today? It finds itself in a new historical situation drastically different from earlier centuries. The changes raise questions about both the content of the message and the ways in which it is presented. The present study is primarily concerned with the second aspect. By what practices and structures today can the Church reach clarity on the meaning of the gospel and announce it in words and deeds?

Why raise this question in the context of the ecumenical movement? Three major reasons may be mentioned:

1. The churches differ deeply in their understanding and in their practice of authoritative teaching. In the course of history, they have developed different concepts, ways and modes of teaching. Thus, they start from different historical presuppositions as they seek to appropriate and to transmit the apostolic truth today. If they are to advance on the road to the unity of the Church, these different approaches need to be clarified and reconciled.

2. Today all concepts, ways and modes of teaching are being tested. Many churches are experiencing that their inherited practices of teaching are now no longer operative. The problems they face in the contemporary world require not only new answers, but also new ways of answering. The ecumenical movement may provide them with the opportunity of sharing their difficulties and engaging in a common search for new and

1

more adequate approaches to their task.

3. Finally, the question also arises because the fellowship among the churches is growing. Obviously, they are not yet sufficiently united to speak authoritatively with one voice, but increasingly there are occasions when they are capable of bearing common witness; and even if they continue to teach separately, it is becoming more and more recognised that each church, in its teaching, needs to take into account the teaching of other churches.

These three considerations are more fully discussed in the three sections of this paper.

The title of the study has sometimes been misunderstood. A few explanatory remarks may help to clarify the intention of the study.

(a) Although the title asks the factual question as to how the churches *do* teach today, it should be clear that the study does not exclusively aim at a description of ways and modes of contemporary teaching by the churches. An adequate analysis of the present situation is of decisive importance for the mutual understanding among the churches, but ultimately the study seeks to answer the questions: How *can* and *should* the Church teach authoritatively today?

(b) The study is primarily concerned with the corporate aspect of teaching. How should the *Church* teach in order to guide its members in the truth and to give witness to the gospel? Obviously, attention is also paid to the witness of individuals and groups as it contributes to and depends on the Church's teaching, but the primary focus remains the representative teaching of the Church.

(c) The title may give the impression that the Church must necessarily engage in acts of formal teaching, but the term 'teach' does not intend to prejudge the ways in which the Church has to transmit the gospel today. It is used in a wider meaning and stands for the multiplicity of ways in which the Church as a community communicates authoritatively the apostolic truth to its members and to the world—statements, models of action, forms of worship, and so on.

(d) The term 'authoritatively' indicates that the attention of the study is primarily directed at authoritative acts of teaching. The Church teaches 'authoritatively' when it claims to interpret authentically today the apostolic tradition as witnessed to the Scriptures and the creeds as well as in the whole life of the Church. Ideally, authoritative teaching will be also authentic teaching. It must be recognised, however, that there may be a tension between authority and authenticity. Teaching proclaimed 'authoritatively' by the Church can turn out to be untrue (sometimes even after having been enthusiastically received). Authenticity depends on the inspiring and sustaining power of the Spirit. This does not mean that the Church should cease to teach authoritatively. It lives under the promise of the Spirit; strengthened by this promise, it will constantly seek to prepare for authentic teaching. The present study is meant to help in this task.

1. DIVERGENCES AND CONVERGENCES AMONG THE VARIOUS TRADITIONS

The various confessional traditions differ greatly in their ways and modes of teaching. In order to advance to a common understanding, these divergences need to be seen clearly. How does each church approach its task of teaching authoritatively today?

(a) Authoritative teaching: past and present

As they seek to interpret authentically today the apostolic tradition, all churches refer to the past. What has been taught authoritatively in the past provides guidance for the task which the Church is called to fulfil today. Scripture, the ancient creeds, the ecumenical councils, the great church fathers, and the Church's experience have all played a formative role in shaping the teaching which is accepted as authoritative in the various churches, even though each church places different emphases on these factors. Yet, the Church cannot teach authoritatively today by simply repeating the authoritative teaching of the past. The churches all recognise the need to continue to teach when faced with new questions which call for a decisive response. Such teaching can take different forms. Some churches have promulgated new dogmas or confessions of faith, others have sought to provide an authentic explanation of the apostolic tradition by interpreting or re-interpreting the teaching of the past which is recognised as authoritative by the Church. Varying degrees of authority are attributed to the different forms of continuing teaching.

(b) Continuity in authoritative teaching

All churches affirm the necessity that the ongoing teaching of the Church, in whatever form it takes place, must be in continuity with the apostolic tradition. All teaching must be based on the *memoria* of God's great deeds in history. Radical departure from or discontinuity with the apostolic witness is rejected by all churches.

How is continuity to be understood? Here the traditions differ. Some admit the possibility of developments, changes and even apparent contradictions; others reject in principle any form of discontinuity. Therefore, what appears to some Christians to be a necessary organic development is deemed discontinuity by others.

Inevitably, all traditions recognise that, in the course of the centuries, there have been shifts or modifications. There are at least three different approaches to the relationship between continuity and discontinuity.

(i) Some would claim shifts and modifications have been at a lower level of change in terminology, practice and structures. They posit an original purity and completeness of a deposit of teaching which can be preserved through the ages with minor adjustments.

(ii) Others recognise that there have been real shifts in teaching, but see these as harmonious developments or organic growth.

(iii) Still others maintain that the discontinuity goes further. In order to make the gospel actual or contemporary, the teaching of the past may need to be recast. They see continuity rather in the liberating message of the gospel than in the various teachings in which this message has been actualised. In their opinion, when new situations arise, teaching practice and structures of the Church may need to change. Only the demands of the gospel can determine what must be retained and what must be altered for the sake of faithfulness.

(c) Who teaches in the Church?

All churches agree that the ongoing teaching of the Church, which is not simply a repetition of the past, is necessary to fulfil the Church's mission to communicate the gospel to the world. The ongoing teaching is a response to questions raised in the encounter between Church and world. Each act of ongoing teaching must be rooted in the whole people of God. It has its starting point in the consciousness of the Church and must be received by it; but there are persons or groups who have to fulfil specific roles to bring it about.

At various times and in various ways, the following exercise functions in the ongoing teaching of the Church.

(i) Church members who have *personal credibility* by their words and actions as 'communicators' of the gospel, like saints, monks, theologians, founders of spiritual movements or even churches, church-reformers. Many of them exercise a prophetic function in the Church.

(ii) Church members, who have *ministerial authority* to preach and teach in the Church, to administer the sacraments and to oversee the community in order to keep them faithful to the gospel: pastors, priests, bishops and other church leaders.

(iii) Representative gatherings within the churches, like councils, synods, bishops' conferences and others, which exercise a *corporate teaching authority* in the Church.

All churches recognise the need for all or several of these roles in one form or another. They differ considerably, however, in understanding their nature and their weight; they also hold different views on the relationship between them and on the way in which the whole people of God need to be involved in the various stages of ongoing teaching. In any case, teaching must be appropriated by the whole people of God.

It is important to distinguish between an anticipatory role in the ongoing teaching of the Church and the formal decisions taken by representative offices or bodies. Saints, prophets, theologians, small communities, and so on sometimes anticipate the teaching which the Church, through its representative instruments, makes its own only at a later date. It is crucial for the teaching of the Church that such voices be heard and heeded; room should be left for creativity and courageous prophecy in the Church.

Some kind of ministerial teaching, some pastoral authority, preserving and promoting the integrity of the *koinonia* in order to further the Church's response to the lordship of Christ and its commitment to mission, is equally indispensable for the Church. They discern the insights of the believing community and give authoritative expression to them, sharing its quest for understanding the gospel in obedience to Christ and receptive to the needs and concerns of all. Such a function of oversight (*episcope*) is present in most churches, although opinions differ on its forms and structures.

(d) Authenticity in teaching

How does the Church acquire certainty that what is being taught is in authentic agreement with the gospel? Obviously, all churches insist on the need for conformity with the witness of Scripture and tradition. Can further criteria for certainty be given? The answers of the various traditions differ in their emphases.

(i) Some, while not excluding other authorities, emphasise the authority which is inherent in a certain office. If the bearer of that office has spoken, the teaching can be trusted as truth.

(ii) Other traditions emphasise the role of confessional documents as an important means of safeguarding the authenticity of teaching.

(iii) Other traditions have difficulties in accepting as criteria either the authority of an office or confessional documents. In their view, there cannot be any criterion for authenticity outside the consciousness of the whole people of God. Teaching proves its authenticity by being received and appropriated by the people of God, living in conformity with the gospel, celebrating the Eucharist and fulfilling its prophetic and priestly calling in the world.

(iv) Others still, while not denying the need for an office or the value of confessional statements, insist on the role of every community and every believer in verifying the authenticity of the teaching which is offered. Every community and every believer has finally to judge for themselves whether or not the teaching is conformable to Scriptures as they understand them.

Can the ecumenical movement, by bringing together churches with different ways of verification, lead to a more comprehensive approach? Can churches be strengthened in their witness by the teaching of another church, even if that church has received it as authoritative in a way which differs from their own? Can the churches, by striving to perfect their ongoing teaching within the framework of their tradition but in dialogue relation to each other, move step by step to greater unity and thus reflect more fully the catholicity of the Church?

2. TEACHING AUTHORITATIVELY TODAY

As the churches seek to respond to the contemporary world, often the inherited ways and modes of teaching prove to be inadequate; they are led to adopt new approaches. What are the main characteristics of these shifts? Three aspects may be mentioned here:

(a) The variety of situations

Both in content and in style, the teaching of a church will be influenced by the situation in which it lives. Today, there is a clearer awareness of the immense variety of situations which the churches have to face. In order to reach a common understanding of the Church's task of authoritative teaching, a careful analysis of this variety is required.

In the eyes of many, the variety constitutes a threat to the teaching of the Church; the teaching seems to fall apart into teachings which arise from the various contexts. In fact, this is not the case. The variety rather manifests the richness of the tradition as well as its capacity to respond pertinently to different situations. The sharper awareness of variety raises, however, in a new way the question of the relationship between teaching addressed to the whole Church and teaching formulated on behalf of the whole Church in particular situations.

(b) Authority in Church and in society

Styles, ways and modes of teaching in the Church are influenced by patterns of authority in society. Teaching processes in the Church must then be seen in relation to the situation in the societal context.

Sometimes structures of authority in the Church are a conscious or unconscious reflection of the structures of authority prevailing in society. For instance, in many churches the emphasis on the role of synods is partly due to the rise of democracy; in many African independent churches the role of the leader corresponds closely to that of the local chief.

In many cases, the Church will seek to adapt its style of teaching in order to be better heard in society. In societies which place primary emphasis on action and achievement, it may seek to teach through practical commitments and programmes rather than through statements, and the like. In other cases, it may develop its style of teaching in opposition to the values prevailing in society. For instance, in the authoritarian society it may emphasise freedom and participation in the decision-making processes; in a society dominated by structures of injustice it may be led to a critical revolutionary approach and develop a style of teaching which seeks to manifest the identification with the oppressed classes.

Often patterns of teaching in the Church which have legitimately evolved at a certain point of history continue to be used, even if in the meantime the situation in society has changed. For a long time, for instance, the Church maintained concepts of authority which corresponded to the mentality of a feudal society. Sometimes churches, without abandoning their earlier theories about teaching, adapt their teaching processes *de facto* to the requirements of the times. For instance, many churches of congregational type have *de facto* developed new structures at regional, national and universal levels.

Special attention needs to be given to the impact of modern media of mass communication; in some countries they play a considerable part in the life of the Church. But the churches are not yet accustomed to making appropriate use of them in their teaching. Sometimes the vacuum of authority which churches leave is filled by the influence of the mass media. Ways should be found for mass media to serve as means of responsible participation of the whole community.

(c) Towards new patterns of credibility

How to teach with authority today? For the faithful and effective exercise of the Church's teaching authority, four aspects require special attention today.

(i) *Change:* Today, most churches are much more sharply aware of the changes having occurred in human society and affecting the life of the Church. They realise, therefore, that teaching may need to be adapted to the needs of the present time. While in the past identity with the earlier teaching was considered to be the mark of truth, more and more the churches are coming to the conclusion that faithfulness to the apostolic truth requires a new presentation of the gospel. Change, which used to be regarded as innovation and betrayal, can, in fact, be faithful witness to the past.

Teaching will always aim at enabling the Church to fulfil its calling to the world, to enter into meaningful dialogue with specific partners, to discern and interpret new perspectives in history, to denounce evil, and so on. Teaching will take place in constant interaction with the world.

(ii) *Pluralism:* More and more, plurality in teaching is no longer seen by the churches as necessarily illegitimate. Positions which used to be regarded as contradictory are no longer considered as necessarily mutually exclusive. A new appreciation for the richness of aspects in the Bible and the vast variety of situations is emerging.

The growing variety of interpretations may cause the problem of diffusing the visible unity of the Church's teaching and call into question the Church's identity. The acceptance of pluralism does not necessarily militate against unity. Authoritative teaching should seek to maintain the Church in unity, yet not impose uniformity nor deny creative difference. The oneness has its primary root in the Eucharistic fellowship and in the common mission and witness of the Church.

Obviously, pluralism must not be misunderstood as 'indifferentism' or 'relativism'. The Church must also know how to say 'no'. Faithfulness to the apostolic witness implies that there may be unfaithfulness. Obedient listening and the desire to teach aright call for the recognition that sometimes the line between truth and error must be drawn. The churches cannot teach authoritatively unless they recognise that they are not automatically preserved from heresy.

In this context, the question arises to what extent some forms of discipline in matters of faith and morals are necessary in the Church. If there are juridical structures regulating such discipline, they should be strictly subordinated to the calling and mission of the Church and not allowed to deteriorate into juridicism, limiting the freedom of conscience of individual church members and ministers. Disciplinary measures which may be necessary to maintain the clarity of the Church's message must not contradict the ethos of freedom which is characteristic of the New Testament.

(iii) *Participation:* Today, there are signs in many churches that more people are participating in decision-making processes. Theologians are often asked to advise bishops or synods; leaders of local churches share to a larger extent in the procedures of teaching at the universal level; more frequently the actual experience of parish priests is taken into account by synods; local communities share in shaping catechetical material.

Such participation is theologically based on the fact that the gift of the Spirit is given to the whole Church and that, therefore, the discernment of truth needs to take place through the interaction between all its members. Participation is a way of expressing the *sensus fidei fidelium.*

(iv) *Reception:* In many churches there is today a stronger emphasis on the need for reception of teaching by the whole Church. Reception is another aspect of participation. To the degree in which teaching has been arrived at through the participation of the entire body of Christ, reception will be facilitated. Structures of participation at all levels of the Church prepare the way for reception.

The term 'reception' must not be taken to imply that decisions are arranged 'from above' and then simply submitted to the community for passive 'reception'. Reception is not only official endorsement, but also a profound appropriation (*Aneignung*) through a gradual testing process (*Bewährung*) by which the teaching is digested into the life and liturgy of the community.

Ultimately, authoritative teaching is always an 'event' which happens and cannot be organised or programmed, juridically or structurally. The authority of the Church is based on the authority of God and his design for the world in Jesus Christ; it depends on the gift of the Spirit. The teaching of Jesus was authenticated by his deeds and miracles. So, too, the Church's teaching will be authenticated by the blessings of the Spirit, not by 'persuasive words of wisdom, but by the manifestation of Spirit and power'.

3. AUTHORITATIVE TEACHING IN THE CONTEXT OF THE ECUMENICAL MOVEMENT

Though still differing in their understanding of the Church and its unity, the churches have been able to describe at least in outline the goal they are committed to achieve together. The Fifth Assembly of the World Council of Churches in Nairobi offered the following statement on the 'unity we seek':

The one Church is to be envisioned as a conciliar fellowship of local churches which are themselves truly united. In this conciliar fellowship, each local church possesses, in communion with the others, the fullness of catholicity, witnesses to the same apostolic faith, and, therefore, recognises the others as belonging to the same Church of Christ and guided by the same Spirit. They are bound together because they have received the same baptism and share in the same Eucharist; they recognise each other's members and ministries. They are one in their common commitment to confess the gospel of Christ by proclamation and service to the world. To this end, each church aims at maintaining sustained and sustaining relationships with her sister churches, expressed in conciliar gatherings whenever required for the fulfilment of their common calling.

The fellowship among the churches today is still preliminary and 'preconciliar', but it anticipates and heralds the future goal. The churches are called to advance step by step to full conciliar communion. In particular, through their acts of teaching they should prepare the way to that unity which is capable of common conciliar decisions.

Often the churches, afraid of possible divergences in their ranks, tend to withdraw from authoritative teaching. They try to preserve peace and unity by avoiding critical issues rather than by taking positions on matters of faith and justice. But there is no escaping. They need to hazard peace and unity and dare to confront error and unrighteousness. Controversy within the Church and conflict with evil in the world may be inevitable if the Church is to be faithful to its Lord.

How can the churches, in the ecumenical movement, assist each other to teach more effectively in fidelity to the apostolic heritage of the Church?

B

(a) Common teaching today

(i) *Acts of common teaching:* Despite their doctrinal differences, the churches often find themselves capable of teaching together. They may be able to formulate together catechetical material. They may be able to offer guidance on crucial issues facing the society in which they live. In particular, common corporate acts of witness become possible when the churches respond to the need of identification with oppressed people. As they seek to manifest the liberating power of the gospel in solidarity with suffering humanity, they will find themselves bound together by their witness.

The need for common teaching exists equally in each country. Churches should seek, therefore, to formulate together the authoritative witness required in their situation. Often guidance on new pressing issues arising from the encounter with the contemporary world can more easily be worked out at the international level and provided through the common witness of the churches. In order to respond adequately, some distance from immediate national interests is sometimes needed, and furthermore there are occasions when a wider range of competence is required than is at the disposal of any individual communion. The World Council of Churches and other ecumenical bodies have therefore a special responsibility in formulating common Christian teaching on such issues in order to encourage, stimulate and guide the churches in their teaching. Studies, statements, recommendations and actions on such issues as peace, race, human rights, the use of nuclear energy, and so on are thus important means to help the churches in their task.

(ii) *Sharing in the teaching of other churches:* Today, teaching is necessarily taking place in fellowship with other churches. Churches can be strengthened by acts of teaching offered by other churches. Churches whose simplicity of teaching has been shaken can rejoice in the straightforward witness of other churches. Those yet undisturbed in the inherited expression of the Christian faith can learn from others to seek new styles of witness and life. New understanding and commitment may come to the whole Church through the creative encounter between the younger and older churches.

The sharing can take place through explicit acts:

(α) In some cases, churches may find themselves stimulated to associate themselves with the teaching of another church on the meaning of faith. A participant from the GDR was able to offer the following example. The Synod of the Roman Catholic dioceses in the GDR issued in 1974 a statement with the title 'Faith Today'. A committee of the Federation of Evangelical Churches in the GDR decided to examine this document and to ask whether the witness of this Roman Catholic text can be considered by the Evangelical Church as an adequate 'Account of Hope' for our time. The committee has worked out a statement which offers a positive evaluation of the document as well as a number of critical remarks. The work was guided by *three* main *questions*: (*a*) Does the document adequately reflect the centre of the biblical witness? (*b*) Does it repeat doctrines considered by our Fathers as deviations from the gospel to such an extent that communion was excluded? (*c*) Does the document make concessions to the spirit of the contemporary world, to the demands of today's society and dominating ideologies which obscure the meaning of the gospel? The committee said 'yes' to the first and 'no' to the second and third questions and, therefore, despite some critical reservations, it was able to see in the document, 'Faith Today', the witness of Christian brothers and an expression of the common Christian hope.

(β) When Christians denounce injustice in dangerous circumstances, they are acting on behalf of all churches. Their action is a call to other churches. They should declare their support for their witness across confessional boundaries. An example for such support can be found in the recent statement of Baptist ministers in El Salvador associating themselves with a group of Jesuits who had taken a courageous political stand; the statement is particularly important because, going beyond the immediate powers of support, it seeks to challenge the inherited patterns of Baptist hostility towards the Roman Catholic Church.

(γ) Often, teaching in a particular situation is of significance beyond the boundaries of the country and requires a response from other parts of the ecumenical fellowship. In this respect, the World Council of Churches has a special task: it should fulfil a mediating role by bringing the efforts and achievements (as well as sometimes the failures) of the churches in one place to the attention of the churches in other places and offering them the opportunity of a response.

(iii) *Sharing in the witness of saints and martyrs:* The life and death of extraordinary witnesses have an impact which reaches far beyond confessional boundaries. In a real sense, it could be said that personalities such as Dietrich Bonhoeffer or Martin Luther King do not belong to one church, but to all churches. Though not explicitly, they are implicitly recognised by them as their own.

Of course, the formal recognition of saints poses serious problems which cannot easily be solved. But there can be no doubt that saints and martyrs in past and present may witness to Christ in a way which transcends the divisions; they often express the deepest content of the Christian tradition. For Christians, the cross of Christ is the supreme act of identification with suffering humanity. Those who die for Christ testify in a special way to his liberating power. The testimony of a martyr is thus always a call to all churches; each can be enriched by knowing of those from other churches who have died for the cause of the gospel.

(b) Common teaching and 'visible unity in one faith and one Eucharistic fellowship'

In order to advance towards unity in one faith and one Eucharistic fellowship, conscious actions by the churches are required. Through the ways and means of authoritative teaching which are at their disposal, they need to promote the movement to the goal. For this process, the following suggestions may be offered.

(i) Multilateral agreements like the agreements on baptism, the Eucharist and the ministry have a special role in the process. They provide a framework within which the churches can undertake their initiatives towards unity. The decision of the Fifth Assembly of the World Council of Churches to submit the agreed statements to all churches for their considered response indicates a clearer recognition of this interaction between theological work and church response. In the light of the responses received, further theological work will need to be undertaken. Consensus can only be reached in stages.

(ii) Responses to multilateral agreements should be sought both at the level of confessional traditions and at the level of regions, nations and local churches. In their response, confessional traditions should facilitate the growth of communion at all levels.

(iii) In the light of multilateral agreements, the churches of one region should work towards consensus on faith, taking into account the special confessional constellation and the special historical and cultural conditions of their regions. The elaboration of common responses would provide an opportunity to work out ways of teaching together and of developing the possibility of common acts of teaching in today's world.

(iv) Churches should associate representatives of other churches at all stages with their decision-making. Such presence can take different forms: observers, consultants, participants without vote or even with vote. In some cases, joint sessions of decision-making bodies may be possible.

(v) In order to make decisions representative, the community as a whole should be part of the process. Churches will need, therefore, to promote responsible discussion of ecumenical findings within their own ranks.

The present practice has many unsatisfactory aspects. Often, ecumenical findings are published without clear address and definite indication about the response expected. They exercise a certain influence, especially in countries where the public means of communication contribute to their dissemination, but they are not taken up by the churches in 'concerted action'. This very easily leads to a tension between an 'ecumenical atmosphere' and the life of the churches as expressed by church authorities.

(c) A new self-assessment in the perspective of the ecumenical movement

As the churches engage in the ecumenical movement, they need to re-examine deliberately their ways and modes of teaching. Consensus and communion in conciliar life can be reached only if the ways of teaching become more and more capable of common decision-making. At present, the response of the various churches to ecumenical findings both of multilateral and bilateral conversations have very different status. While in some churches a response by the authorities does not commit the church, in other churches it would have so much weight that the authorities prefer to refrain from responding. In order to make consensus real in the churches, the weight of decisions needs to become comparable.

Bas van Iersel

II. Who according to the New Testament has the say in the Church?

IT IS, of course, not possible to find in the New Testament a direct answer to the question as to who has the decisive say in the Church, even if we were to transpose that question back into the past and confine it to the period in which the New Testament texts were written. We are not, however, entirely in the dark here. It is true that the question is never formally raised, but directions and indications are given here and there with regard to the taking of decisions or the factual or ideal procedure in decision-making is described. It is therefore possible, by using these data, which can be found in Matthew, the Acts, the epistles and the Apocalypse, to trace the answer that would be most closely in accordance with the New Testament if the question were asked: Who was permitted or had to have the decisive say in the Church?

This implies that the question as to who had the say in the Church is clearly a limited one. It would require more space than I have at my disposal to investigate which persons had the right and the duty to raise their voices to proclaim the message, to teach, to bear witness, to confess, to accuse, to comfort, to spur on, to prophesy and to speak in tongues. That is why I propose to confine this article to the simpler question as to who, according to the New Testament, had the authority to make binding pronouncements. If I am not mistaken, however, I am in so doing concentrating on the question under discussion in this issue of *Concilium*.

1. THE GOSPEL ACCORDING TO MATTHEW

Matthew's is in fact the only gospel in which the word *ekklēsia* occurs (16:18; 18:17) and the question about authority to make decisive statements is raised. In Matt. 16:19, Jesus tells Peter that what he binds or looses on earth will be held as bound or loosed by God.[1] This statement is repeated in almost exactly the same words in 18:18, but in the second case it is applied to all Jesus' disciples or even to the *ekklēsia* in general.[2] There is, after all, a discussion in verses 15-17 about the procedure that should be followed if a brother has sinned and the ultimate decision rests with the *ekklēsia*, which is, in this context, the local community. It is only if we were to fail to read on after 16:18-20 that we might make the mistake of thinking that only Peter and his successors were permitted to make decisive pronouncements. It is not difficult to find a large number of objections to

11

this view, the five most important being, in my opinion, the following.

(a) If the gospel of Matthew was written after Peter's death, he had become invisible as the foundation. This is a characteristic of all foundations—seen in time, they are situated in the past.

(b) This foundation was a rock for a very good reason. A rock foundation is unique and sufficient in itself. It is firm enough to bear the complete building, however large that building may become. For this reason, Peter, as the foundation, has no successor and the function of the rock cannot be transferred.

(c) The power of the keys can, however, be transferred as the authority to open and close, to bind and loose. This power is transferred to the *ekklēsia*, the assembly of the brethren. Jesus is in their midst even if there are only two of them, although his assistance presupposes a gathering.

(d) Later in the gospel, an unfavourable judgment is passed on a structure in the Church in which individuals in authority are able to make decisions. In 20:25-28 and 23:8-12, on the other hand, it is stated emphatically that Jesus' Church is a community of brothers (and sisters in 12:50) and that no one is greater than another in that community. Only one distinction makes a member of the community stand out above the others—a greater readiness to serve.

(e) In accordance with this, the part played by Peter in the gospel of Matthew is more modest than that in the other gospels. What is particularly striking is that he is not mentioned at all in the stories about Jesus' resurrection. He is not distinguished in any way from the other brothers (28:10), the ten other disciples (verse 16).

An *answer* to our question, then, that corresponds to this view would run something like this: A leader does not have the authority to take important decisions alone; that power is shared by the whole assembled community. What should take place if the community does not reach a consensus of opinion is not clear. The justification of this power is to be found in the bond with Peter and through Peter with what the Father in heaven has revealed about Jesus and what Peter as the spokesman of the brethren has confessed.

2. THE APOSTOLIC COUNCIL OF JERUSALEM (ACTS 15)

Acts 15 contains an account of how an insurmountable difference of opinion about whether circumcision was necessary for salvation was resolved. The community at Antioch was not able to reach a decision itself and a delegation was sent to Jerusalem with the task of obtaining a binding statement. If this account is compared with the account of the meeting at Jerusalem in Gal. 2:1-10, in which the delegate Paul gives his view of the matter,[3] a large number of problems arises.[4] I will therefore take the safest point of departure, namely that Acts 15 is not a factual account of what happened, but an account that was modelled by its author and adapted to the place and the function that it had in his book. Two aspects of the account as it appears in Acts 15 are, in my opinion, exceptionally important.

The first is the way in which the decision comes about within the framework of the account. According to Gal. 2:6, 9, the 'pillars' of the Jerusalem community, James, Cephas and John, made the statement, whereas, according to Acts, this statement was made in a larger assembly. Initially, only the 'apostles and elders' are mentioned (verse 6). In verse 12, the expression *pan to plēthos* is used. This may have several meanings. In Luke 23:1; Acts 23:7, it means 'the whole assembly'. In Luke 19:37; Acts 5:14, it means 'the whole multitude' and, in Acts 6:5; 15:30, it may mean 'the whole community'. In our present context, what is clearly suggested is that an extended company, if not the whole community was present. The addresses are followed by the account of the decision-making process, which begins with the words: 'Then it seemed good to the apostles and the elders, with the whole church. . . .'[5] The author keeps clearly to the idea that the decision can only be made if the whole community is present and involved in it.

The second important aspect relates to the extent of the decision taken. The matter is placed before the assembly at Jerusalem by the community of Antioch, to which town the letter with the decision is sent (verses 22, 30-31). The letter is, however, addressed to the brethren 'who are of the gentiles in Antioch, Syria and Cilicia' (verse 23). According to Acts 16:4, Paul and Timothy had the decision made known in the cities of Lycaonia and Pisidia during a second journey, in this way extending it far beyond the sphere of those to whom it was initially addressed. In 21:25, the letter has clearly become an encyclical to 'the gentiles who have believed'. The decision of the Jerusalem community was in this way given a lasting and more universal validity and the status of Jerusalem as the mother-community, where decisions that were binding on all other communities were taken, was stressed. Jerusalem was, after all, the place where Jesus' resurrection was first proclaimed (Luke 24:47-48; Acts 1:8) and where Peter, James and John could be the guarantors of the bond with what had been said and done by Jesus himself in the city, in Galilee and on the way to Jerusalem.[6]

We can say, then, that the *answer* provided in Acts to the question as to who has the authority to make binding pronouncements is similar to that found in Matthew. That answer is that a binding decision can only be taken when the whole community is involved. The wider power of Jerusalem to make decisions is legitimated by a reference back to the original Christian witness borne to Jesus and indirectly to the event of Jesus himself.

3. PAUL AND THE CORINTHIAN COMMUNITY

Paul occupied a unique position and had exceptional authority in the communities that he founded. It was he who planted and built (1 Cor. 3:6-10; 2 Cor. 13:10). It was he and he alone who, through the proclamation of the gospel, begot the community and its members and who was among them as a father and his children (1 Cor. 4:14-17; 2 Cor. 6:13; 1 Thess. 2:11; Philem. 10) or even as a wet-nurse (1 Thess. 2:7) or a mother (Gal. 4:19). It would hardly have been surprising if he had exercised his authority paternalistically or at least individualistically, but it is clear from his epistles that he did not and especially from those addressed to the community in Corinth.

It is not difficult to discern from the objections that were raised to the way in which he made his authority felt (2 Cor. 10:1-10; 13:1-10) that he did not act as a 'strong man' and that he did not want to appear in that light. Even though he had at times—and was sometimes asked—to settle disputes (see 1 Cor. 7:17; 11:17, 34; 14:40; 16:1), he never wanted to act as someone who was lord and master over the faith of others (2 Cor. 1:24). It therefore made a great difference to Paul whether or not there was, in a given matter, a commandment of the Lord (1 Cor. 7:6, 10-40; 9:14; 14:37; 2 Cor. 8:8-10). In faithfulness to what had been handed down to him (1 Cor. 11:2, 16, 23; 15:3; 2 Thess. 2:15; 3:6), he always passed on any such commandment in such cases. If he was unaware of any such commandment, it was not his practice to impose one himself and thus fill the gap. On the contrary, he simply gave his opinion (*gnomē*, 1 Cor. 7:25, 40; 2 Cor. 8:10). It is clear, then, that he himself took quite seriously what he had written in 1 Cor. 10:15: 'I speak as to sensible men; judge for yourselves what I say'.

Paul did not behave as a man who had the right to say the last word. If there had to be a 'last word', he preferred to point to the 'first word', that is, to the gospel or to a word of Jesus. If there was no need for a 'last word', then he would give his opinion—with or without the support of arguments—and leave it to the community to draw its own conclusions or to reach a decision.

There are at least two cases in which it is clear that he did in fact leave the decision to the community. He wrote about the first in 1 Cor. 5:1-13,[7] a passage in which he criticises the Corinthian community for having failed to take measures in a scandalous case of sexual immorality and tells the members to take measures at once. A great deal in this passage is obscure,[8] but there can be no doubt at all about the answer to the question as to who, in Paul's view, should formally take the decision. His personal point of view is quite clear. It is that the person concerned should be punished. But he does not impose the punishment himself. On the contrary, he calls on the community to exercise its authority in an assembly and to punish the man. It is quite important that there are striking similarities between this passage and Matt. 18:15-20, both as far as the subject-matter and as far as the vocabulary are concerned.[9] These show that, both in theory and in practice, there was more agreement between different communities than there would appear to have been to judge from the meagre and disparate data available.

The second incident is discussed in 2 Cor. 2:5-11. The subject-matter is similar to that of the first case, but, because the man who was punished had repented, Paul calls on the community to forgive him. There are three important matters in this passage. First, it is quite clear from verse 6 that the punishment was imposed by the community as a whole. We may therefore conclude that an assembly of the kind recommended by Paul in 1 Cor. 5:4, was not an unusual incident, but a normal procedure. Second, it is probable that verse 6 refers to a decision by the community that was taken with simply a majority of votes. This is only a possibility, since the words *hoi pleiones* can be translated in several ways. In my opinion, however, the most obvious translation is 'the majority'.[10] In that case, it should be clear that the community also took majority decisions in the absence of unanimity. The third important fact in this passage is this. In verse 8, the community is urged to 'make a decision' (*kuroō*). This is a juridical term and its use points to the fact that this passage is concerned with a formal procedure of decision-making.[11]

We may therefore conclude that, in this case too, it is the community and not an individual official that has the power to make decisions and that these decisions can be made by majority vote if the community is not unanimous.

4. UNDER A PSEUDONYM

With regard to the question as to who had the authority to make binding pronouncements, there are also relevant data in the pastoral letters, the Catholic epistles and the Apocalypse. There are many texts in all of these documents in which false teachers are criticised. This criticism is sometimes general, but it is difficult to escape the impression that the authors of the texts usually had particular men in mind (see, for example, 1 Tim. 4:1-7; 2 Tim. 4:34; Tit. 1:10-16; 2 Pet. 2:1-22; 1 John 2:18-27; 4:1-6; 2 John 7-22; Jude 3-16). Names are mentioned in other texts. One Diotrephes is mentioned, for instance, in 3 John 9-10. This man's fault was apparently to take it on himself to expel members who did not want to dance to his tune from the community. It is obvious that the author of the epistle disapproves of Diotrephes' behaviour, but his precise objections and why he has them remain obscure. Certain false teachers are mentioned by name in 1 Tim. 1:20—Hymenaeus and Alexander, who is also named in 2 Tim. 4:14-15 as a difficult customer—and in 2 Tim. 2:16-18—Hymenaeus and Philetus. These men are not, however, condemned in the epistles. Apparently they had already been condemned previously.

Compared with what we have so far established with regard to the New Testament, a deviant picture is presented by the pastoral epistles. In 1 Tim. 1:20, the author states that he has delivered Hymenaeus and Alexander to Satan. This terminology is reminiscent of 1 Cor. 5:5 and because of this similarity in terminology the difference is all the more striking. In the letter to the Corinthians, Paul was calling on the community to carry out this punishment, whereas in the pastoral letter the author appears to have carried it out personally, that is, individually (like Diotrephes?). A similar approach can also be found in other texts. The instructions about prayer in 1 Tim. 2:8 begin, like the conclusions about the position of young widows (5:14) with the words: 'I will' (*boulomai*). What the author of the epistle to Titus writes to the latter also points to a similar arrangement, namely that Titus should warn a heretic twice and then expel him from the community (Tit. 3:10). It is clearly an individual action, rather than one undertaken by the whole community, and is therefore a procedure that is different from that encountered in the other texts that we have considered.

The information given in Apoc. 2:1-3:22 is in accordance with the procedures described elsewhere. These two chapters include the letters to the seven churches in Asia Minor, in which the author appraises their position. One of his criteria is their attitude towards the Nicolaitans and their false teaching, something about which we know nothing. The church at Ephesus is recommended for its members' hatred of this teaching (2:6). The churches of Pergamum (2:14-16) and Thyatira (2:20-23), on the other hand, are rebuked because they allowed the Nicolaitans complete freedom in the community instead of combating their teaching. It is very unlikely, but the phrase 'the angels of the churches' (2:1, 8, 12, 18; 3:1, 7, 14) may possibly point to officials in the churches. If it does not, then, as in 1 Cor. 5:1-13, the whole community and not a single church leader is made responsible for removing the false teachers.

I have placed all these texts together under a single heading, which I have entitled 'Under a pseudonym'. I cannot unfortunately discuss in this article which of these writings was in fact written under a pseudonym,[12] but there can be no doubt that at least some of them were. This is quite important in connection with our theme. In particular, the choice of the pseudonym is significant. In the case of proper names, these are Paul, Peter, James, John and Jude. The last also points indirectly to James, because he is presented as the latter's brother (Jude 1:1). It can hardly be a matter of pure chance that, apart from the reference to Paul, they should all point to the three pillars of the Jerusalem church (see Gal. 2:9), who also had a privileged place in the synoptic tradition with regard to contact with Jesus.[13] In my opinion, this whole question is connected with the legitimation of authority by pointing back to the origin. This is a phenomenon that is also encountered in Matthew, Acts and the Pauline epistles.

5. CONCLUSIONS

With the exception of the pastoral letters, the image presented in the New Testament is unexpectedly and strikingly homogeneous. In matters of doctrine and morals, the assembled community and not individual officials in the community is ultimately responsible for making decisions. There is even possibly a trace in the texts that we have considered of a procedure in which decisions are taken by majority vote in the absence of unanimity. The legitimation of this authority is based, in various ways, on a reference back to the origin of Christianity.

The pastoral letters, on the other hand, almost unquestionably make officials in the churches responsible for these decisions. This inevitably gives rise to the question as to whether the procedure in these letters should be regarded as a model to be followed later in the Church or as an exception to the general rule. It would only be possible to answer this question within a wider context. I am of the opinion that a synodal model of the Church is more in accordance with the New Testament and that the pastoral letters here provide an exception to the rule.[14]

Translated by David Smith

Notes

1. See B. Rigaux 'De heilige Petrus en de hedendaagse exegese', *Concilium* 3, 7 (1967) 135-166; R. Pesch 'The Position and Significance of Peter in the Church of the New Testament' *Concilium* 4, 7 (1971) 21-35; J. Blank 'The Person and Office of Peter in the New Testament' *Concilium* 9, 3 (1973) 42-55; C. Kähler 'Zur Form—und Traditionsgeschichte von Mt 16, 17-19' *New Testament Studies* 23 (1976-77) 36-53; F. Hahn 'Die Petrusverheissung Mt 16, 18f' *Wege der Forschung* 189 (1977) 543-563; P. Hoffman 'Die Bedeutung des Petrus für die Kirche des Mattäus' in J. Ratzinger *Dienst an der Einheit* (Düsseldorf 1978) pp. 9-26, in which other books and articles are listed.

2. The distinction between authority with regard to doctrine (16:18-20) and discipline (18:15-17) that is sometimes made seems to me to lack sufficient motivation.

3. See T. Holtz 'Die Bedeutung des Apostelkonzils für Paulus *Novum Testamentum* 16 (1974) 110-149.

4. In addition to T. Holtz, *op. cit.*, see also C. Talbert 'Again: Paul's Visits to Jerusalem' *Novum Testamentum* 9 (1967) 26-40; D. Catchpole 'Paul, James and the Apostolic Decree' *New Testament Studies* 23 (1977) 428-444.

5. It is clear from the vocabulary that at least verses 22-23a in this passage were the work of the author. R. Morgenthaler *Statistik* pp. 181-182, believes that *agō, anēr, pempō* and *sun* were preferred in Luke and Acts, *kaleō* was preferred in Luke alone and *adelphos, dia, ekklēsia, Paulos, presbuteros* and *cheir* were preferred in Acts alone. The impersonal use of *dokeō* only appears in Luke 1:3; Acts 15:22, 25, 28 (34); 25:27; Heb. 12:10. There are ten cases of *ho kaloumenos* with a proper name in Luke, thirteen in Acts and three in Revelations. *Dia* with the genitive of *cheir* only occurs in Mark 6:21; Acts 2:23; 5:12; 7:25; 11:30; 14:3; 15:23; 19:11, 26 and *holē hē ekklēsia* only occurs in Acts 5:11, where it refers to the Jerusalem community; see, however, 1 Cor. 14:23.

6. This is presumably why the relationship between Paul and Jerusalem was emphasised in Acts. A stay in Jerusalem is constructed in Acts 9:26-30 that is in conflict with Gal. 1:17. In Acts 22:17-21 (see 26:16), there is an account of Paul's vision in the Temple during this visit to Jerusalem, which would appear to be a formalisation of the vision on the road to Damascus.

7. See J. Cambier 'La chair et l'esprit en I Cor. V.5' *New Testament Studies* XV (1968-69) 221-232; J. Murphy-O'Connor 'I Corinthians, V, 3-5' *Revue Biblique* (1977) 238-245.

8. Not only the offence, but also the precise nature of the punishment in verse 5 are not clear. A physical punishment would seem to be the most obvious, but, together with Cambier, *op. cit.*, I think that excommunication is more likely.

9. With regard to the vocabulary, I would point to *adelphos* in Matt. 18:15 and 1 Cor. 5:11; *sunagomai* in Matt. 18:20 and 1 Cor. 5:4 (a *hapax legoumenon* in Paul) and the apposition *eis to emon onoma* in Matt. 18:20 and *en tōi enomati tou Kuriou Iēsou* in 1 Cor. 5:4; possibly also *ekklēsia*, which is very rare in Matthew, but especially frequent in 1 Corinthians, where it occurs 22 times.

10. A different translation is preferred in Zorell's dictionary, the grammar by Blass, Debrunner and Rehkopf and the commentaries by Thrall (1965) and Bruce (1971). The translation 'the majority' is preferred in the following commentaries: Bengel (1773), Plummer (1915), Allo (1937), Lietzmann and Kümmel (1949), de Boor (1972), Bultmann (1976) and Wendland (1978). Bauer mentions both possibilities in his dictionary, but does not state a preference.

11. This is Behm's view; see *Theologisches Wörterbuch zum Neuen Testament* III pp. 1098-1099.

12. This is the opinion of F. Laub 'Falsche Verfasserangaben in neu-testamentlichen Schriften' *Trier Theologische Zeitschrift* 89 (1980), 228-242, with further bibliography.

13. For example, about 110 names are given of Christians in the New Testament, about 85 of them men. In principle, each of these 85 should be regarded as pseudonyms.

14. See B. van Iersel 'Structuren van de kerk van morgen' *De toekomst van de kerk*, an account of the World Congress of *Concilium* in Brussels, 12-17 September 1970 (Amersfoort and Bussum, 1970) pp. 116-126.

Boris Bobrinskoy

III. How does the Church remain in the truth?

1. An Orthodox Response

1. TRUTH AS THE ECCLESIAL REVELATION OF THE LOVE OF THE TRINITY

(a) The Church established and judged by the truth

AT THE end of the twentieth century, as the essentials of the Christian faith are being called in question (the divinity of Christ, his resurrection, his presence in the sacraments, the authority of the Church and authority in the Church and man's own divine vocation), it is necessary to ask whether the Church is still able to perceive the truth, to transmit faithfully the gospel message of salvation and to defend and protect this deposit of faith through the centuries against distortions, reductions and heresies.

The truth which Jesus reveals to us in his own person is a living truth, in other words, the final reference, the supreme stability, the basis of all human speech and language. In his work of salvation Jesus reveals to us God's infinite love and draws us into it. The Spirit of truth, the Paraclete, ensures the faithfulness of the transmission to men of God's own love and makes that love living, true and fruitful.

The Church is the place above all where the Spirit blows and where Christ lives, he who is the wisdom and power of God. St Paul rightly calls the Church 'the pillar and bulwark of the truth' (1 Tim. 3:15).

But the Church does not possess the truth as something which belongs to it. On the contrary, it is rooted in the truth, by Jesus' express promise, to the end of the ages (Matt. 16:8; 28:20; John 14:16). But while the Spirit lives in the Church and gives it life and vigour, the Church is not guaranteed against errors and infidelities. Its dependence on and fidelity and obedience to Jesus is continually renewed in a permanent attitude of *epiclesis*, of invocation of the Spirit of truth who lives in the Church, renews it but also judges it (Rev. 2-3).

(b) Liturgical celebration of the truth

(i) The Church's prayer and liturgy express and manifest its essential identity and its vocation in human history. It is because divine truth is the perfectly holy Trinity itself

18

giving itself to men to lead men to itself that truth is celebrated, sung, praised and invoked. There are not two different languages for speaking to trinitarian truth and proclaiming it to the world. That is why theology is by nature 'doxological'; it implies praise, liturgy, prayer, and sanctification. But, in its turn, the liturgy is full of theology; it breathes theology. This is the fundamental experience of the Orthodox Church. Its liturgy is nourished by theology, but it also inspires all the steps the Church takes in theology.

In its liturgical worship with the Eucharist at the centre, the Church celebrates revealed trinitarian truth. It makes a 'memorial' of the works of God in the history of salvation and, by the invocation of the divine Spirit, it makes the events of salvation present here and now, makes us contemporaries of the Jesus of history and of the Lord of glory.

But the liturgical celebration of trinitarian truth overflows the temporal and spatial limits of liturgical worship. Or, rather, the liturgical celebration of truth never stops because it continues in between the Sunday liturgies in the permanent witness and preaching of the truth without which the Church would cease to be the Church. But celebrating truth before the face of God and proclaiming it to men stem from a single action, a single inspiration, a single sanctifying impulse of the Spirit. That is why St Paul refers to the preaching of the gospel to the pagans as a liturgy and talks about it in liturgical terms (Rom. 1:9-15). Similarly, at the very heart of the sacramental action of baptism and the Eucharist, we find the trinitarian confession of faith, which is set out in the baptismal professions of faith and in the 'eucharistic prayers' (see B. Bobrinskoy 'Confession de foi trinitaire et consécration baptismales et eucharistiques dans les premiers siècles' in: *La Liturgie, expression de la foi* (Rome 1979) pp. 57-67).

In the liturgy the praise and memorial of the Trinity unfold. This communion in the truth overflows the framework of worship and is continually renewed and developed in the hearts of the faithful when, at the end of the Eucharist, they are sent out into the world (*Ite missa est*, 'Let us go in peace') to bring to it the living truth which lives in our hearts.

(ii) In this way the Church exercises a real priesthood in the world. The proclamation of the truth, its defence and its constant clarification themselves stem from the three-fold ministry of Christ which continues in the Church. *Priesthood* is the liturgical celebration of the truth and its proclamation in the world. *Kingship* is light's struggle with and victory over darkness, a permanent struggle in which the light of Christ forces untruth and sin to come out into the open (*Oportet et haereses esse*, 1 Cor. 11:19). Finally the *prophetic ministry* of the truth is both the witness of the eternal word in the power of the Spirit and suffering to the point of martyrdom for that truth which the world cannot receive.

2. THE DOCTRINAL MAGISTERIUM OF THE CHURCH AND IN THE CHURCH

(a) The Church in permanent council

It is because the Church is engaged in a continuous celebration of the divine Trinity through the rhythms and alternations of worship and its intervals (for example Sunday and the week) that it is by nature conciliar and its liturgy places and keeps it permanently within the domain of the divine Trinity's own eternal concelebration.

Councils do no more than express and manifest in an exceptional way this conciliar, collegial nature of the Church, that miracle always impossible but always repeated of inner unanimity and the resulting instinct or inner feeling for the truth. It is because truth is alive and present in the Church that it is expressed and formulated spontaneously through the *magisterium*; it is not the *magisterium* which creates, imposes or infuses it into a Church which lacks it.

I want to insist on this *instinct for truth or instinct for orthodoxy in the people of God*, in the ecclesial body as a whole. This has been a fundamental idea in Orthodoxy in every age, and it provides ample explanation for the stubborn resistance of the Orthodox people through the centuries to the western 'innovations' over the Filioque or infallibility, or to the reductions performed by the Reformation on the very mystery of the Church, its divine and human structures, its sacraments, the veneration of the saints, etc.

In addition to the 'non-theological factors' which may have played a part in the antagonisms between West and East, I am convinced that in all its resistance and all its rejections Orthodoxy has been motivated by a fundamental concern for the fullness and wholeness of the salvation of man and the world.

(b) The hierarchy's doctrinal magisterium

We must now consider the exercise of authority in the Church and the regulative function of the hierarchy in matters of faith and doctrine.

To describe the Church as being in permanent council means that the Church retains as its primary criterion the first Pentecost assembly, when the Spirit rested on the apostolic community and established it in the truth and in love. The apostolic preaching shot up spontaneously from that ecclesial Pentecost and that preaching formed the first exercise and manifestation of the apostolic function of the Twelve in the Church. The whole of the New Testament shows us the development of the Church around its source in that apostolic preaching, which very soon became part of the Church's canonical books. The apostles' concern for the fullness of the truth and its preservation from errors and divisions is constant and clear.

This concern for truth, for orthodoxy, runs through all the work of the apostolic age. St Irenaeus of Lyons was one of its most authoritative representatives when he described the march through space and time of truth and tradition, which never loses its original identity, and marked the boundaries between the apostolic tradition and heresy. It is finally to the bishops that the charism of truth (*charisma certum veritatis*) has been entrusted; they, as successors of the apostles, have to defend, proclaim and transmit it in the churches for which they are responsible.

(c) Ordinary and extraordinary ministry

From the origins of the Church the proclamation and defence of the faith have been an essential responsibility of the hierarchy. The ordinary expression of these duties was in liturgical preaching and baptismal catechesis, and it is certain that these have been marked, through the ages, by the doctrinal conflicts which have shaken the Church.

Very early, even in its beginnings, the Church encountered distortions of the faith, which were a source of suffering to it. The concepts of heresy and the heretic are correlative to and inseparable from that of orthodoxy.

Throughout its history the Church was forced to define its position in the face of old or new heresies which shook it, but also forced it to make an effort to reformulate fundamental theological truths. The mystery of the Trinity, God and the world, man and his divine vocation, the mystery of Christ, true God and true man in a single person, the veneration of icons, the uncreated energies of God at work in the divinisation of man. Today it is the mystery of the Church, the communion of saints, the veneration of saints and prayer for the dead.

While the modern ecumenical movement has profoundly altered the climate of relations between separated Christians and has contributed to the creation of a new climate which is more authentically irenical and more propitious to a genuine fraternal dialogue, the problem of safeguarding the fullness of the faith still remains grave and urgent. Today as in the past, doctrinal pluralism, like diversity in liturgical and sacramental rites, has its limits and accordingly the idea of heresy remains as a boundary which theological reflection may not cross without—not simply incurring canonical or disciplinary sanctions—but calling in question the very truth and fullness of the salvation brought to us in the Church.

The normal, permanent exercise of the hierarchy's doctrinal *magisterium* remains one of the most constant norms of ecclesial life. When doctrinal disputes spilled over the boundaries of the local church it became necessary to summon regional or universal councils. The latter never possessed 'infallibility' as such; this is an idea which has no place in traditional Orthodox ecclesiology. On the other hand this in no way detracts from the full significance of the truths of faith proclaimed by these councils, but it is always within the Church that these truths are alive and that the post-conciliar process of 'reception' of conciliar decisions takes place, a fact to which the whole history of the ecumenical councils bears witness.

3. THE EXERCISE OF THEOLOGY IN THE CHURCH

(a) Theology, the baptism of intelligence

It is important to recall the communitarian and ecclesial character of theological activity. Theological knowledge and theological language are inseparable from their goal, the mystery of God. Intelligence has to undergo a sort of baptism, dying to the old man and the sinful categories of our fallen world in order to reach knowledge, the rebirth of the new man, renewed according to the stature of the fullness of Christ. Theological knowledge (and theological research) is thus inseparable from the spiritual experience which transcends individual limitations and is lived in the Church and its communion. That is why the practice of theology is itself ecclesial, communal, and why the process—a sacramental process—of the testing of the theologian's theological activity and its reception—always critical—by the Church must also take place in the Church and according to the Church's sacramental and hierarchical structures. This process of reception is essential to the life of the Church and manifests the life of the Spirit in the Church. It may be fast or slow. It may include contradictory periods, the temporary rejection of the truth in favour of heresy (Arianism, iconoclasm—and their modern reincarnations), and may lead to the martyrdom of confessors of the faith (St Maximus the Confessor) or to their banishment from the community of the Church (St John Chrysostom, St Symeon the New Theologian, Maximus the Greek).

(b) Theological research

The question of theological research, its legitimacy and its criteria and limits, has revived in our own day a debate which has gone on in the Church in every age. It is the duty of theology to express the faith held from the beginning, to record it and formulate it; but do not heretical distortions or innovations compel theology to probe doctrine more deeply, with new words and new demands? Did not the disputes about the Trinity and Christology in the period of the great ecumenical councils lead to a renewed vision of the mystery of the Trinity and the Christological dogmas? The impact of this on the Church's piety was enormous.

Finally, the constant activity of mystical authors such as Gregory of Nyssa, Symeon the New Theologian or Gregory Palamas led to a genuine theological synthesis by taking the main results of conciliar theology and situating them more firmly than ever in the context of a deeply authentic and lived spiritual experience.

But it is always the Church which receives, tests, discerns and recognises the authenticity of any theological language or system. There is no 'independent theology' outside the Church. Even the spirit of prophecy is obedient to the Church (1 Cor. 14:32).

On the other hand, the Spirit which inspires the prophets may lead them to pass a judgment on the Church (Rev. 2-3). The theologians must therefore be humble and attentive in the face of this truth which he proclaims and probes and by which he is judged. Truth protects itself and provokes reflexes, reaction, refusal, rejection. Even here, however, the Church applies the discernment of the Spirit to its own exercise of discernment, to distinguish proper motives of rejection from improper ones (fear, fanaticism, obscurantism or pastoral care for the flock, etc.). If then theological research is carried out in the Church, for it, for its witness, the Church's doctrinal *magisterium* must be exercised by the normal or extraordinary means by which the bishop, in union with his people, carries out his responsibility for the integrity of the faith and of its transmission. *In Orthodoxy, however, there are no external criteria or infallible guarantee of the truth of its members.* Still less can there be question in the Orthodox Church of an 'ecumenical *magisterium*' in the sense of a higher and wider authority which could decide in the last resort on the orthodoxy of this or that doctrine.

CONCLUSION

The conclusion of this article may seem disappointing to readers in search of infallible guarantees or methods. The Spirit of truth lives in the Church and gives it life. He renews the Church's structures, purifies its piety and clarifies its language. He makes that language adequate and appropriate to its object, which is the holiness and glory of the Triune God acting in the world.

But through the vicissitudes of its history the Church rediscovers the energy of its youth when it learns once more not to possess anything but to receive everything from the Comforter, the Spirit whom it invokes, receives and transmits. It is in this way that the Orthodox Church lives, as a gift constantly renewed but never acquired or possessed, *unanimity of faith in essentials, liberty in secondary matters and in all things charity.*

Translated by Francis McDonagh

Ulrich Kühn

III. 2. A Lutheran Response

(a) The position of the Reformers

A BASIC insight of the Reformers in their sixteenth-century dispute with the Church authorities over the truth can be formulated by saying that there is as yet no definitive guarantee by a formally legitimated teaching authority that the Church remains in the truth. Even those endowed with teaching authority in the Church can fall into error, and indeed even councils can err.[1] And it is the job of the entire Christian community to pass judgment on the teaching that takes place in the Church.[2] The conviction of the Reformers is that the Church remains in the truth if it remains true to holy scripture and to the word of God attested in it. The point of the Reformers' insistence on *sola scriptura* is to exclude every purely private opinion in the interpretation of scripture and to allow the authority of scripture itself to come into play both against the individual ideas of the interpreter and against everything that in the Church's prevailing understanding can obscure what it has to say.[3]

These statements are indeed critical with regard to a Church teaching authority. But they do not exclude the Reformation being aware of the necessity of Church teaching. The gospel attested to by holy scripture is indeed really oral proclamation.[4] An inalienable mark of the Church is that in it the gospel is 'taught' by people called to do this.[5] Beyond this the Lutheran Reformation recognises a form of the control of teaching to be seen to by the bishops. According to article 28 of the Augsburg Confession among the duties of bishops is 'to judge teaching and reject that which is against the gospel'.[6] With regard to the teaching of the Church even councils are accorded a necessary function by Luther: their job is to pass judgment according to the standards of scripture in disputes that may arise.[7] Luther valued highly what the four earliest councils had done in this regard and considered it authoritative for the Church.[8]

In this way the Reformers themselves were not prepared to go any further than an abstract *sola scriptura* but saw Church structures that went beyond this as necessary if the Church was to remain in the truth.

(b) Credal statements in the Lutheran Church

As early as the sixteenth century a further factor was decisive for the Lutheran churches that emerged and developed. This was the statements of belief that were brought together in the Book of Concord in 1580. Increasingly in the Lutheran church the Church's persistence in the truth was understood as adherence to the credal statements of the Reformation (and those of the early Church). A particularly central and fundamental role in this was played by the Augsburg Confession of 1530.[9] Alongside holy scriptures, the Lutheran confessions of faith provide the doctrinal basis in the Lutheran churches, until the present, a basis that is also legally binding.[10] This 'confessional status' is usually asserted in the preambles to the constitutions of Lutheran churches and in some cases is undergirded by prescriptions ensuring that the statement of faith remains unaltered and that its contents cannot be the object of Church legislation.[11]

But scripture and statement of faith cannot simply be equated, and this finds expression in the difference in terminology used in many constitutions. Thus it can be said that the gospel is 'given' in holy scripture and is 'attested' in the statements of faith.[12] This terminological differentiation recalls the explicit provisions of the Formula of Concord and thus of one of the basic confessional documents. In its introductory article 'On the guiding principle and rule of judgment' it makes plain that 'holy scripture alone' is 'the only judge, rule and guiding principle' in the Church, while 'the other confessional statements . . . and writings referred to . . . merely bear witness to and explain the faith' and indicate how holy scripture was interpreted in earlier times and false doctrine guarded against.[13] Subsequent Lutheran dogmatic theology draws a corresponding distinction between the *norma normans* (scripture) and the *norma normata* (confessional statement). This distinction pays tribute to the reformation doctrine of *sola scriptura* but does it in such a way that the confessional statements have the status of a Church-approved guide to the appropriate interpretation of holy scripture. In this sense the ordained ministers of the Lutheran churches are obliged to regard scripture and confessional statements as the foundation and standard of their preaching and teaching, while those 'who are placed in the Church for spiritual oversight' have to make sure that this obligation is kept to.[14]

(c) The problems that arise from Lutheran practice

Problems needing further consideration and solution are thrown up by the outlines that have been sketched out above of the responsibility for doctrine in the Lutheran churches.

The many differing and conflicting ways in which scripture and confessional statements can be interpreted in preaching and teaching and which have in quantity and quality reached an extent hitherto unknown[15] give a quite new urgency to the question of what really matters in the Church, what the Church today teaches as binding and essential.[16] Clearly simply pointing to scripture and to the credal statements of the past is not enough. The Church needs to give new answers, new joint statements need to be made in which the voice of the gospel is formulated today in the sense of a 'communal linguistic ruling'[17] binding on all, as a consensus of the Church.

A further challenge is represented by the ecumenical encounter of the churches. The statements of faith that have come down from the sixteenth century for the most part formulated the teaching of the Lutheran church in the context of controversy aimed at marking the distinction from other churches. But over recent decades it has become increasingly clear that the history of the Church, of belief, and of theology over the past four centuries, and not least the ecumenical contacts and encounters that have taken place, have themselves led to developments and changes in people's awareness of what they believe; and these have opened up the possibility of formulating the belief of the Lutheran church today in such a way that decisive points of convergence with other churches and their basic dogmatic beliefs become visible. This conclusion, with all its implications for the relationship of the churches to one another, does however entail binding doctrinal decisions at some time or another, perhaps in the form of a formal acceptance of the results of ecumenical dialogue.

But the Church's past confessional statements that have been handed down to us require re-interpretation, just as holy scripture does, quite apart from the arguments that have been mentioned. What they say is to a considerable extent imprisoned in the questionings and the conceptual world of the sixteenth century and must be made accessible once again for the Church of the present day.[18] This of course is continually happening in practice in the preaching of the word of God and in theological research and teaching. It also takes place in the form of official Church guidelines and memoranda on questions of the day. But this does not add up to official Church teaching. The development of official doctrine in the Lutheran churches has not got beyond the sixteenth century and is in Church constitutions tied to the situation prevailing at that time. To a certain extent this is comparable with the situation in the Orthodox churches, whose officially valid doctrine is limited to the decisions of the early councils. Even the Barmen Declaration of 1934 and the Leuenberg Agreement of 1973 are not recognised by the Lutheran churches as a real advance in the formulation of their belief.[19]

Clearly this is an unsatisfactory state of affairs. As the community of those who pass through history under the guidance of the apostolic word the Church needs valid official doctrine accepted by everyone as the expression and assurance of their joint hearkening to scripture and of their common confession of their faith in past and present. But this doctrine should not simply have the form of ancient confessions of faith that have been handed down from the past. Rather, if it is not to smell of the museum (and thus to be treated in practice by many as purely of historical interest), the confession of faith dating from an earlier period needs to be carried forward dynamically and 'brought up to date' by the Church's confession and consensus in the new historical situations that arise, just as happened, at least in embryo, at Barmen in 1934.

2. CONDITIONS FOR THE CHURCH TO REMAIN IN THE TRUTH

A Lutheran answer to the question 'How does the Church remain in the truth?' has to include the lasting conclusions of the Reformers in its consideration of how the Church today can measure up to the task of providing a binding teaching. Here we can only indicate a few conclusions, almost in the form of theses, drawn from the material that has already been presented.

(*a*) The Church remains in the truth if the spirit of God, in keeping with his promise (see 1 Tim. 3:15), maintains it in the truth. It is possible and indeed necessary to talk of an 'inerrancy' of the Church even on the basis of Lutheran and Reformed theology.[20] But this 'inerrancy' is *not to be firmly and definitely tied to any ecclesiastical institution*. The Reformation remains correct in asserting that there is no institution in the Church, including a council, where it can be guaranteed that nothing but the truth will occur and be articulated and for which under certain conditions the predicate of 'infallibility' can therefore be claimed *a priori*.[21] The Church's persistence in the truth, despite all the human effort that is needed to ensure suitable structures for searching for the truth, is ultimately a gift of the Spirit of God which is not at the Church's disposal.

(*b*) The Church remains in the truth if it remains true to the biblical witness, allows itself to be guided to the understanding of this witness by the voice of the Fathers of the Church, and thereby stands in agreement with the Church throughout the centuries. The fact that holy scripture is primarily to be interpreted by itself does not therefore exclude the *existence of a common tradition of hearkening to scripture* stretching back and forward throughout the history of the Church, a tradition that for its part has normative significance for the Church today. Nevertheless this consensus is only the touchstone for the truth to the extent that it can be seen in the light of scripture as the latter's accurate and factual interpretation.

(c) The Church remains in the truth if it once again makes the witness it has inherited of scripture and Church teaching its own in the conditions of the present and gives it new expression. This kind of contemporary 'teaching' by the Church can take several forms:[22] various kinds of preaching and proclamation that touch people's hearts and minds and, possibly through prophetic admonition, build up the body of Christ; theological teaching as the outcome of methodically disciplined reflection on the origin, history, contents and expression of Christian belief; and in particular cases when a suitable *kairos* of confession or awareness on the part of the Church arises, it can take the form of an ecclesiastical consensus which formulates what the Christian community can today confess and express jointly and in a binding manner. What occurs in all forms of Church teaching is the process of 'translation' of the message handed down in scripture and tradition into contemporary terms, a process that starts in the New Testament itself.

(d) The Church remains in the truth if in particular it has at its disposal suitable means for forming and maintaining a consensus and 'sound doctrine' within the Church. What is fundamental in this respect is the comprehensive *process* of a *communicatio fidei*[23] within and between the individual churches. This is a process of a multilateral exchange of views both inside and between the various churches involving bishops, synods, professional theologians, ordained clergy, other church workers, and ordinary congregations. The involvement of the local community or congregation in this process of forming and maintaining the Church's doctrine is an important and fundamental principle of the Reformation, and it is of particular significance today in view of a widespread difference in awareness between ordinary Christians and Church leaders. On the other hand, however, in a certain contrapuntal divergence from the kind of internal problem facing the Catholic Church, the responsibility of the bishops for doctrine needs to be developed by extrapolating from the prescriptions of article 28 of the Augsburg Confession: it should perhaps be described as a special responsibility for the unity and common sharing of faith and doctrine within a region of the Church and between the various churches. In this an essential element remains the 'conciliar' tying-in of the bishop's authority within the individual churches and in the ecumenical realm. Open dialogue is needed precisely at the point where for the sake of preserving the unity of the faith a first step towards separation presents itself as unavoidable.

(e) The Church remains in the truth if it lives on the basis of the truth. At its deepest level the truth that the Church teaches and confesses means a way of life that springs from him who is 'the truth and the life' (John 14:6). Truth that is taught in the Church is genuinely binding only to the extent that it is the *expression of truth that is lived*, the expression of 'testimonies before kings' (Ps. 119:46), and the expression of the service of love. This is shown in a special way in the consensus of the Church. The process of reaching consensus demands listening to each other, being open to correction on all sides, sharing in questioning and seeking, respect for other people's opinions, but also brotherly discussion and disputation: in a word, even the process of reaching a consensus within the Church, or rather precisely this process, must take place on the basis of love. Here too above all the extent is clear to which the Church only remains in the truth if it is led by the spirit of God.

Translated by Robert Nowell

Notes

1. See Martin Luther, Weimar edition (WA) 1:656; 39:I:185.

2. See Luther's tract *Das eine christliche Versammlung oder Gemeine Recht und Macht habe, alle Lehre zu urteilen* of 1523, WA 11:408 ff.

3. Holy scripture is *sui ipsius interpres*, WA 7:97; see G. Ebeling *Wort Gottes und Tradition* (Göttingen 1964) p. 125.

4. See Luther, WA 10:I/1:626.

5. See Augsburg Confession, article 7.

6. Augsburg Confession 28:21.

7. WA 50:615.

8. See the tract *Von den Konziliis und Kirchen* of 1539, WA 50:488 ff.

9. See for example *Die Bekenntnisschriften der Evangelisch-Lutherische Kirche* (reprint of the 1930 edition) pp. 5 ff.

10. In many Lutheran churches not all the documents collected together in the Book of Concord share the same authority.

11. See for example article 3:3 of the constitution of the Evangelical Lutheran Provincial Church of Saxony of 13 December 1950 (as revised 11 April 1960).

12. As for example in the constitution mentioned in note 11.

13. *Die Bekenntnisschriften . . .* (note 9 above), p. 769.

14. As in the declaration on doctrinal obligation and the use of doctrinal authority issued by the United Evangelical Lutheran Church of Germany (VELKD), 16 June 1956. On this see 'Wie lehrt die Kirche heute verbindlich?' (edited by Ulrich Kühn) in *Die Zeichen der Zeit* (1978) no. 9, pp. 321 ff.

15. See Karl Rahner *Schriften zur Theologie* IX, especially pp. 12 ff.

16. See the first part of the as yet unpublished report of the working party on the Church's binding doctrine which was put before the synod of the Federation of Evangelical Churches in East Germany in September 1980.

17. Karl Rahner *Schriften zur Theologie* V, p. 68.

18. Efforts to achieve a hermeneutics of dogma that do justice to the subject are further advanced in Catholic than in Protestant theology.

19. In the context of the acceptance of the Leuenberg Agreement there was a debate over the question whether a Lutheran church had any right at all to make a decision affecting the confessional status in this way, and it was established that the Agreement did not rank as a confessional statement. The Barmen Declaration (or the various repudiations of it) may be mentioned in Lutheran church constitutions but not in the context of describing the Church's dependence on the sixteenth-century confessional statements. The situation is different for example in the Evangelical Church of the Union.

20. See Hans Küng's idea of talking about the Church's 'indefectibility' or 'perpetuity in truth' *Unfehlbar? Eine Anfrage* (Einsiedeln 1970) pp. 148 ff. (ET *Infallible? An Enquiry?* London 1971 pp. 150 ff.).

21. The real problem for Protestants trying to understand the doctrine of infallibility is the possibility of *a priori* infallible propositions, not the Church's being preserved in the truth: see also O. H. Pesch in *Papsttum als ökumenische Frage* (Munich/Mainz 1979) especially p. 209.

22. On what follows, see the report mentioned in note 16 above, sections 3:1 and 3:4.

23. See A. Houtepen ' "Lehrautorität" in der ökumenischen Diskussion: Verbindliches Lehren der Kirche heute' in *Ökumenische Rundschau*, supplementary number 33 (Frankfurt 1978) 140 ff., 179 ff.

Harry Kuitert

III. 3. A Reformed Theologian's Response

THIS ARTICLE is not concerned with profound expositions of the truth or of the Church but represents the simply formulated opinion of a Reformed theologian as to how the Church can sustain the truth. There are many Reformed theologians and, consequently, many opinions, but this is mine and I intend to argue in its favour as well as possible.

1. THE REFORMED ANSWER

To begin with, let us cast our minds back to the times when life within the Church was still fairly straightforward. Reformed Christians also experienced these times but there are few of them left today. This is, perhaps, an oversimplification of the matter which everyone will recognise.

The question of how the Church sustains the truth was answered by Reformed protestants in referring to the Holy Scriptures as the *suprema iudex controversiarum* (the highest judge in matters of doctrinal dispute). Calvin already pointed in that direction and Reformed scholasticism of the eighteenth century showed it even more clearly. I am leaving the question of whether this led to a prevailing view of the Bible which greatly differs from that of Luther and in a lesser degree from that of Calvin. I am referring only to the fact that the Bible was considered to be the highest court of appeal in virtually all ecclesiastical disputes, since controversies about Church-ordinance and liturgy were also looked upon as doctrinal disputes. Thus one expected, and indeed tried, to maintain the truth in the Church and to sustain the Church in the truth.

Yet another fact can be noted, namely that the model used in this discipline was known, attractive and convincing. It was provided by the Church of Rome from which one had turned away. There the institution of the papal authority had the 'last word'. Criticism by both Reformed and Lutheran Protestantism was concerned not with the model itself but with its application. Papal authority was replaced by the Scriptures. Thus it was possible to refer to a 'last word' which was not just a 'word' spoken by a human being but the word of God Himself. Those were the days when mockers within the Protestant camp called the Bible 'the paper pope'. Those days are now over.

2. THE PROBLEM

(a) The Historicity of Scripture

No longer does Reformed Protestantism use the Bible so readily as the 'final judge in doctrinal disputes'. The hermeneutical problem in all its facets has come to light, viz., there is an historical distance between the world of former times and that of today; at what point can we say that we understand a text; do these texts have a meaning for us or do we give them a meaning? In a few words, the faith of Reformed Protestantism in the Bible has been shaken by a flood of questions. The inevitable outcome has been that the Bible is now seen as a 'human' book containing, among other things, a great number of prescriptions which we do not follow, even though they have been laid down by God. On the other hand, many of the things we do practise are not to be found in the Bible.

I am referring to this development not because I wish to expand on it, but in order to demonstrate that for Reformed Protestantism both in fact and in theory the Bible is no longer considered to be the final judge and the 'last word' as it was in the flourishing period of Protestant scholasticism. As a consequence of this at least one of the main stays supporting the controversy between Rome and the Reformation has collapsed.

(b) The Traditional Character of Scripture

We can go even further and draw yet another conclusion which is of no less importance for our subject. Since we have stressed the historical character of the Bible and even talk of biblical writers, the controversy about which came first, the Bible or the Church, has also been settled. Classical controversial theology used to treat the question as a matter of importance, which is the reason why it crops up in all old Reformed dogmatics. The Bible is superior to the Church because the Bible came before the Church. Therefore, the thesis that the Bible presupposes an interpreting congregation was considered to be not only dangerous, because tradition and ecclesiastical authority could control the text, but also incorrect.

Considering the issue today we must admit that the Reformed were not as correct in their opinion as they thought they were.

There is no Bible without a Church that reads and interprets. Indeed, the Bible itself is an historical and historically developed manner of interpreting the experiences of the first generations of Jesus's disciples. Without Church there is no Bible.

(c) No Institutional Guarantee of Truth

However, this does not lead to the conclusion that inevitably, therefore, there is a *magisterium*, personified in the pope, that can pronounce a binding interpretation of the Scriptures. I am not rejecting this conclusion merely because I am a Reformed Protestant, but because it does not seem to be logical to me either. Indeed, classical Roman Catholic theology gives a very complicated and elaborate exposition of the ministry, particularly of the papal ministry. This proves that Roman Catholics also found it difficult to explain to the faithful the tenet that the pre-existence of the Church necessarily leads to the priority of the pope, both in ministry and authority.

I shall, however, not pursue this line either. I have mentioned it only in order to arrive at the position in which we find ourselves today, a position which for Roman Catholics as well as for Reformed Christians is characterised by a certain measure of embarrassment that is mutually recognised.

As the position of the Scriptures has been questioned among Protestant Christians, so the position of the pope's authority has been challenged within the Roman Catholic Church. I am not setting out in detail the discussions which have taken place on this issue within the Roman Catholic community. They are well known, particularly to readers of *Concilium*, a member of whose editorial board (Hans Küng) is a formidable protagonist in these discussions. There are good reasons, therefore, to speak of a mutually admitted sense of embarrassment regarding the authority in the Church. No longer can either the Scriptures or the pope be considered to be the highest authority as was so in the old days. I hope a Reformed Protestant may be forgiven for stating this so freely.

3. REMAINING IN THE TRUTH THROUGH DISCUSSION

What then is the alternative? Or, as this issue of *Concilium* puts the question, how do we maintain the truth in the Church, and thus sustain the Church in the truth, if there is no final authority in the sense of the 'last word' concerning matters of doctrine and life? This question is intriguing for both Reformed and Roman Catholic Christians, because both are equally familiar with a Church structure in which the 'last word' features prominently.

My answer to the question is that we have no means of sustaining the Church in the truth other than by discussion. Not everything can be labelled Christian, hence the term truth, and in order to avoid that error the Christian Church must not resort to the formal authority of Bible and *magisterium* but choose the longer way of discussion amongst its members as to what can and what cannot be called Christian.

(a) Without Self-Legitimation

Since the hermeneutical problem arose, the appeal to the Bible has always meant an appeal to a certain interpretation of the Bible. Thinking in terms of the Bible, therefore, always means thinking in terms of one's own interpretation of it, considering one's own interpretation, not the Bible itself, as the 'last word' and so building up a theology which is self-legitimising. Karl Barth is an example of it.

Rome is a self-legitimising church. All uncertainties which necessarily result from the subjectivity inherent in humanity are eliminated by an authority conferring upon itself the right of such elimination.

Self-legitimation is, however, unacceptable, even though it may be backed up by religious arguments. Perhaps I should say, particularly if it is based upon religious arguments. By accepting the principle of self-legitimation the way is open to each individual and each group of people to present oneself or itself as the 'last word'. Furthermore, if a certain group can also exercise power, whether it be physical or spiritual, to impose itself as being the 'last word', a situation is reached which is incompatible with the Christian Church. A Church community which, by virtue of its authority, imposes the truth upon people and in this way tries to sustain the Church in the truth is already unacceptable on purely moral grounds, which means on grounds holding good for all groups and all people. However, there are also religious grounds which are relevant, and, although I cannot discuss them all in this article, I shall advance one of the most important ones.

(b) Aware of our Incompleteness

Our knowledge, including our Christian knowledge, of God is an incomplete knowledge, as St Paul remarks (1 Cor. 13:9). Why incomplete? Because God's self-revelation in His works is still incomplete. The last word has not been spoken about God and cannot be spoken as long as God has not performed His last deed. That is the reason why human experience is an inherent element of the process through which the

Christian Church acquires its knowledge of God. *Christian doctrine* as we know it is the *result* of *experiences in the past*. Without this doctrine (tradition) Christians remain blind and fail to discover God in His works. However, merely maintaining this doctrine *makes* one blind, turns one's eyes in the wrong direction, towards the theory instead of towards the place of action.

Because the last word has not been spoken about God, controversies are part and parcel of daily life in the Christian Church. We have to learn to live with them as subjects of discussion. In accordance with the Bible (Eph. 3:18) the subject of the Christian faith is *the whole of Christianity*. If in the sixteenth century the authorities had had a better idea of this, they would have respected the views of Luther, Calvin and Zwingli, and have kept them within the Christian Church. This does not mean that the Christian Church knows no boundaries, but it does mean that also beyond these boundaries controversies are possible.

Because, and as far as coercion in the Church is precluded on moral and religious grounds, there are no other ways left to sustain the Church in the truth than the way of discussion. This is not such an imposing means as power or formal authority but, in my opinion, it is the only way in which the material authority of the Christian truth can make demands on people. This way depends wholly on the faith in the strength of the Christian truth itself, the belief that this truth does not need manipulations or weapons of any kind to stand its own ground in the world of today.

Translated by W. M. P. Kruyssen

Stephen Sykes

III. 4. An Anglican Response

THE SHORT answer to this question is contained in the Good Friday Collect for the Church, as prescribed in the *Book of Common Prayer* (*BCP*):

> Almighty and everlasting God, by whose Spirit the whole body of the Church is governed and sanctified; Receive our supplications and prayers, which we offer before thee for all estates of men in thy holy Church, that every member of the same, in his vocation and ministry, may truly and godly serve thee.

The Church is *governed by the Holy Spirit*; but the active fulfilment of the 'true and godly' service of each and every person is essential to the performance of the will of God by the Church. The Collect, it should be noted, is an English version of a Gelasian collect. No originality or distinctiveness can be claimed for it, apart from a certain Reformation emphasis on the words 'vocation and ministry'. Most Anglicans have a rather strong aversion to claiming 'distinctiveness', in the sense of overt difference, for their own communion. Rather they would trust that what is 'characteristic' of Anglicanism is also to be found strongly represented in other denominations.

Nonetheless Anglican history has led to a certain practical distinctiveness of approach to the question of how the Church is maintained in the truth, to which it is the purpose of this brief paper to draw attention.

1. THE ANGLICAN EXPERIENCE OF MINISTERIAL AUTHORITY

(a) Based on the Reception of the Gospel by the Whole Church

By 'ministerial authority' is meant, in accordance with the Collect already quoted, the authority inherent in the ministry of every member of the Church. This authority is based, plainly, on the faithful reception by the whole Church of the gospel of Christ. The whole Church fulfils its authorised service in two major activities, those of praise and of evangelism. In general the offering of praise is provided for by a *Book of Common Prayer* in the vernacular, in which the whole Church, literate and illiterate alike, becomes a community of praise. Evangelism was construed within the context of sixteenth-century Europe largely as a practical activity, the witness of godly life; and instruction in it was undertaken by means of the public reading of the Holy Scriptures ('he that readeth so standing and turning himself, as he may best be heard of all such as are present') and by the provision of a sermon or homily. Praise and evangelism are inseparably linked in the General Thanksgiving ('that we show forth thy praise not only with our lips, but in our lives') and in the first prayer of Thanksgiving after communion, which binds together 'this our sacrifice of praise and thanksgiving' (the whole eucharistic action) with the sacrificial offering of souls and bodies (of the eucharistic community) in service to God.

The Anglican reformers' action in identifying *ministerial authority as a function of the reception of the gospel by the whole Church* is of profound significance. The locus of authority in Anglicanism is the whole congregation empowered with the authority of the gospel, and gathered in *common* prayer to confess their sins, to receive absolution, to pray for each other and for the world, to give praise to God, and to receive the gospel sacraments. This is the basic event from which the people of God take on their character as community.

(b) A Function within the Authority-bearing and hierarchic Community

At the same time there is no reluctance shown, on the basis of this shared authority, to identify different gradations of authority within the community on a frankly hierarchical pattern. But although the ordained apostolic ministry of bishop, priest and deacon is carried over into Anglicanism, it is set in a context which expresses, both in liturgical practice and in Church government, the authority of the whole people of God under the gospel. The place of the gospel is publicly expressed precisely in those parts of the *BCP Prayer Book, Ordinal and Thirty-Nine Articles* which explicitly refer to the authority of the ordained ministry. Articles VI ('Of the sufficiency of the Holy Scriptures for Salvation'), XX ('Of the authority of the Church') and XXI ('Of the authority of General Councils') deny to any ordained person, or body of such persons, the right to require any doctrine to be believed as necessary to salvation which may not be read in Scripture; and since the Scriptures are read to the whole people in their own tongue it is assumed that they will be in a position to judge. At the ordination of deacon, priest and bishop a Bible or New Testament is handed to the newly ordained and authority given to read it, to preach or to administer discipline by means of it. All exercise of authority, therefore, is subject to the publicly available Scriptures, and is bound therefore to be exercised according to an *open* criterion.

The same Anglican documents, it should be noted, plainly anticipate that authority will be exercised in various matters. The ordained ministry *has* authority (Article XXIII), inasmuch as they minister by the commission and authority of Christ (Article XXVI). It is expected that morally evil ministers will be subjected to the discipline of the Church, and that excommunications will take place, subject to reconciliation by penance and re-reception by an authorised judge (Article XXXIII). To the Church as a whole is attributed the right to decree traditions and ceremonies in matters indifferent, subject as ever to Scripture and the principle of edification (Articles XX and XXIV). Controversies about particular points in the faith are expected to arise, and bishops are specifically asked whether they will seek a true interpretation of the Scriptures when controversy arises, and exercise discipline according to their scripturally bestowed authority. Priests and deacons undertake reverently to obey their 'Ordinary, and other chief Ministers unto whom is committed the charge and government over' them. On them, in turn, is bestowed the gift of the Holy Spirit by the laying on of hands, by means of which the power of the keys is conferred, and a charge given to dispense the word of God and the sacraments.

In short, there are specific grades and functions within the authority-bearing community. There is a specific, ordained hierarchy; there is provision for the exercise of discipline; there is freedom for churches in different regions to meet local needs and conditions; but there is an awareness of the undesirability of clerical, especially episcopal tyranny, and a clear expectation that argument about the faith will be conducted openly on the basis of Scripture.

2. LITURGY, AUTHORITY, AND DOCTRINE

(a) Liturgy as a conservative force

It is historically evident that one of the intentions of those who decided to impose the *Book of Common Prayer* upon the Church, and require the clergy to use it, and no other book, in the public services of the Church of England, was to protect the people from the private whims and enthusiasms of the ordained minister. Modern liturgical study suggests that the liturgy of the pre-Nicene church was considerably less restricted either by law or by custom, and modern liturgical revision in the Anglican communion has tended to restore the possibility not merely of local variation, but also of a measure of spontaneity in liturgical practice.

Nonetheless it is unquestionably true that the Anglican Communion has a long experience of the power and benefit of an ordered liturgy in the language of the people, and of an ordained ministry disciplined by the canonical requirement that one service book alone defines the liturgical life of the people of God. The *BCP* occupies a still more significant place in the *doctrine* of the Church of England. According to Canon A5 of the same Church:

> . . . the doctrine of the Church of England is grounded in the Holy Scriptures, and in such teachings of the ancient Fathers and Councils of the Church as are agreeable to the said Scriptures. In particular such doctrine is to be found in the *Thirty-Nine Articles of Religion*, the *Book of Common Prayer*, and the *Ordinal*.

The other Provinces of the Anglican Communion either define themselves in the same way, or by explicit reference to the doctrine of the Church of England. In other words, the particular expression of the doctrinal substance of Anglicanism is located largely within the *BCP*. It is apparent that an Anglican response to the question, 'How is the Church maintained in the truth?', must raise the *general question of the relation of liturgy and doctrine*—a question which is very far from being clarified in modern theological discussion.

Liturgy as it is practised by Anglicans is unquestionably a conservative force. It provides a stable central tradition by which Scripture is itself interpreted. It illustrates what might be meant by 'the essentials', without the necessity of a sharp and permanent differentiation from supposed inessentials. It lays heavy emphasis on the continual *anamnesis* of the mighty acts of God, in the context of praise and thanksgiving.

(b) Two objections

Two major objections need, however, to be met.

(i) In the first place, does not the above discussion attribute to an obviously human document, the product of a past age liturgically and theologically, altogether too inflated an authority? This would be the case if the *BCP* was regarded as irreformable. However, it is plain that *BCP* itself envisages *the necessity of revision*, and, since it acknowledges the ultimate authority of Scripture and of such traditions of the ancient Church as are agreeable to Scripture, provides the criteria for its own future revision. Moreover, in practice the Anglican communion has preserved in its experience the successful revisions of 1549, 1552 and 1662; the Scottish and American churches being particularly influenced by the earliest version. Furthermore in recent years Anglican provinces throughout the world have responded constructively to the discoveries of the liturgical movement. A liturgical order is not a new form of 'static' authority, but the acknowledgment of a living tradition of the worship of the God of our fathers in the faith.

(ii) A second objection concerns *the inherent possibility of the ideological subversion of the liturgical act*. A liturgically ordered Church may easily come to believe that its mere recitation of the liturgy is a sufficient fulfilment of its mission. Many Anglicans would today be ready to acknowledge that the preservation of its liturgical traditions has in certain specific cases subserved ideologies of social and racial dominance. The reading of the Psalms, of the Prophets, of the Magnificat, of the Gospel of Luke, or of the book of James has not been sufficient to preserve Anglicans from blindness and hardness of heart. A study of church history as a whole, however, leads one to believe that at no time, and in no denomination, has there ever been immunity from the manipulation of religion in the interest of ideologies of dominance. What the Church needs is critics to unmask falsity and pretence, whose power derives from their appeal to the very documents and standards by which the Church publicly professes to live. Training the Church's critics is an essential element even of the formal public celebration of the rituals of worship.

3. CONFLICT AND MORAL AUTHORITY WITHIN THE CHURCH

The Anglican experience of internal conflict is long and bitter. Throughout the nineteenth century the churches of the Anglican communion were divided on issues of doctrine (especially in relation to the sacraments), of authority (especially biblical inspiration, and the authority of the ministry), and of ritual practice largely of late medieval or Roman origin. In England some of these disputes were conducted in the civil as well as the ecclesiastical courts, and led to deep disgust with 'party' division, and an attempt to find in the concept of the 'comprehensiveness' of the Church a means of transcending the bitterness and triviality of much of the conflict.

The theory and practice of 'comprehension' is now very strongly part of the Anglican ethos, and was specifically invoked at the 1978 Lambeth Conference to interpret and justify the diversity of practice regarding the ordination of women to the priesthood. I have elsewhere argued that the concept is at least ambiguous, and in part dangerous (*The Integrity of Anglicanism*, 1978, ch. 1, 'The Crisis of Anglican Comprehensiveness'); but properly specified it is far from being useless.

(a) A Pattern of Mutually Interacting Elements

The most attractive and important statement of the concept of authority underlying the practice of comprehensiveness is to be found in a Report to the *Lambeth Conference of 1948*, or The Anglican Communion. According to this document authority in the Church is single, in that it derives from a single divine source, but it also reflects the 'richness and historicity' of the Divine Trinity. It is distributed among Scripture, Tradition, the Creeds, the Ministry of the Word and Sacraments, the witness of saints and the *consensus fidelium*. It is thus a dispersed, not a centralised authority. Its different elements combine, interact and check each other. In their plurality lies God's provision against tyranny and the dangers of unchecked power.

Behind this theory lies an interesting historical pedigree. It is, in its main features, the view of authority which characterised that group of Anglican theologians of

Anglo-catholic or high church background who were morally shocked by the Roman treatment of the Catholic Modernists under Pius X. Many of them had links with von Hügel, Loisy or Tyrrell, and shared a number of profound theological convictions in common. The rejection of centralised authority or of unchecked power was precisely articulated by Anglican theologians of the early twentieth century in contradistinction to the way in which Catholic modernism was stamped out. At the same time they clearly affirmed the *authority of the bishop 'in synodical association with his clergy and laity'*, as one indispensible part of the pattern of mutually interacting elements. And what saves the pattern from incoherence or merely random collisions is, according to the 1948 document, precisely what has been insisted on above, namely its fusion in liturgy.

(b) The Difference between Liturgical and Doctrinal Unity

The question naturally arises whether, in fact, there may not be doctrinal conflicts in the Church which are as subversive of its *liturgical* unity, as they would be of its *confessional* unity. In this case liturgy no more provides a fusion of diversity, than does an ambiguous doctrinal consensus. Indeed, in Anglican history liturgy has certainly both produced and sustained some exceedingly sharp conflicts.

It seems, however, that liturgical unity is qualitatively a different kind of unity (or unity-in-diversity) from discursive doctrinal unity, and does not depend on it. *Liturgical unity* exists primarily in the realm of story and symbolic depth; for this reason the narrative of the gospels and the poetry of the psalms are elements of primary significance to the formation of Christian identity. These are the sources of those elemental images which inhabit the Christian consciousness, and do their work in the shaping of Christian character. The Church has no need, and indeed no authority, to go beyond them in discursive precision of expression.

The *conflicts*, therefore, that inevitably arise in the realm *of doctrine or of ethics* generally do so because they are sustainable by the arguments deriving from the very lack of precision inherent in the stories and symbols of Christian faith. Some controversies are based on misunderstandings or faulty reasoning; they have to be answered, and seen to be answered, by a more penetrating examination of the issues. But many more disputes have, in the light of the history of Christian theology, an evidently chronic character, repeatedly breaking out at different periods in slightly differing ways, but exemplifying a consistent pattern of difficulty—as examples, I would name subordinationism in Trinitarian theology, the realist-symbolist distinction in sacramental theology, and the problem of grace and freedom in anthropology. In these cases, there is every reason to doubt forms of argumentation which appear to attribute a uniquely privileged insight into the final solution of the difficulties. Indeed it seems that, inasmuch as these doctrinal disputes are sustained by the internal diversity within Scripture itself, then a liturgically ordered Church which reads the whole Scripture constantly *promotes* internal theological conflict. And in this case it would be an important question to explore what function is served in the very maintenance of the truth by the actual refusal to bring such disputes to premature closure.

(c) Exercise of External Authority

Finally it is plain that the nature of the inward consent to the movement of God's Spirit precludes the exercise of external authority in certain ways. Tyrannous use of authority in the Church is plainly envisaged already by the writer of I Peter. The *BCP Ordinal* sets before the priest, and the whole congregation, a pattern of the exercise of ministry which has its roots in the free growth of the person to the stature of the fullness of Christ. The bishop says to those to be ordained:

> See that you never cease your labour, your care and diligence, until you have done all that lieth in you, according to your bounden duty, to bring all such are or shall be committed to your charge, unto that agreement in the faith and knowledge of God, and to that ripeness and perfectness of age in Christ, that there be no place left among you, either for error in religion, or for viciousness in life.

The words are derived from Martin Bucer, but the Biblical echo is Ephesians 4:1-16, with its model of growth into mature manhood. The concept of maturity has here, as elsewhere in the Epistles, a deeply moral character. No Anglican could possibly pretend that this moral character had not been grievously distorted within the history, including the contemporary history, of his own denomination. Equally no Anglican would allow that the Catholic Church of Christ could set itself any other goal, or seek to protect the truth by any other method, than that which sought to embody this moral character. But whether or not specific acts in the history, including the recent history, of the Christian Church exemplify that character can only ever be itself a matter of moral judgment of a necessarily disputed kind.

Olle Engstrøm

III. 5. A Free Church Response[1]

1. THE TERM 'FREE CHURCH'

THE TERM 'Free Church' is vague and needs some clarification. It could be explained in the negative. Referring to the other responses in this issue of *Concilium*, it would mean *not* Roman Catholic, Orthodox, Lutheran, Reformed, Anglican etc. It should neither be applied to the Methodist tradition with its rather clear set of Church order. What remains might be called Free Church tradition, i.e., Congregational, Baptist and Pentecostal churches and the like.[2]

This definition in the negative also may reflect the historic fact, that most Free Churches have originated in opposition against the existing majority church ('folk church') with its over-inclusiveness and its close relationship to the state. Most of these churches also meant revolt against established church authorities, often with power coming from state legislation.

Free Churches are churches that (*a*) stress independence from state authority; (*b*) hold the view that the Church is the *koinonia* of believers ('the gathered church', the congregation); (*c*) emphasise the freedom of the local church (within a wide range) from radical independentism, e.g., within Pentecostalism to an almost synodical system within certain Baptist and Congregational churches; (*d*) are non-episcopal; and (*e*) non-liturgical (no written liturgy to be followed by all local churches).

2. AUTHORITY IN FREE CHURCHES

As to the problem of authority in the church the following could be said about the Free Churches in general:

(*a*) Free Churches consider '*the Holy Scriptures as the only norm* for Christian faith and its implications in doctrine and life. Within this framework freedom is given to the individual to seek clarity in matters of doctrine and interpretation under the guidance of the Holy Spirit' (from the constitution of the Mission Covenant Church of Sweden). All Free Churches emphasise the ultimate authority of Scripture and tend to hold a rather *biblicistic view* (though ranging from acceptance of historic critical view of the Bible to strict fundamentalism). The full freedom and right of each individual to read and interpret the Bible has had liberating effects for the whole life of the church and was the very basis for the challenge over against established church authorities. According to the conviction of these churches, the Holy Spirit can speak through church leaders, ministers, church assemblies, but also directly to individuals; whose experiences must, however, be shared with and interpreted within the *koinonia* of the local church.

(b) Free Churches have in common a certain *distrust of written, specified credal documents*, spelling out in careful wording doctrinal truths, in the belief that more open, flexible formulations offer greater opportunity for the Holy Spirit to guide and renew, so that new challenges can be met in changing historic situations.

(*c*) No strict distinction is made between a 'teaching authority' (*Lehramt*) in the church and authority in other matters, e.g., policy matters, public statements, administration, etc. *The life of the Church is seen as a whole.*

(*d*) *Neither bishops nor national synods have binding authority* over local churches/congregations.

3. THE CHURCH—LOCAL AND UNIVERSAL

To be able to answer the question, who has the say in the Church, one must know what is meant by 'the Church'.

As has already been said, Free Churches all strongly emphasise the primary importance of the local church.[3] At the very beginning of the history of the Christian Church, it was what happened in the different local places that counted. St Paul's letters to local churches (in Rome, Corinth, etc.) are the strongest indication of the vital importance of the local congregation already in the Early Church. Thus, the basis for the Free Church view in this matter is primarily theological. However, pragmatic and functional arguments are added: in rapidly changing societies of today the local church is the most sensitive part of the Church to new needs and demands and thus also most ready and apt to respond. The local church is the place of renewal.

The relationship between the local and the universal Church (also the very nature of the Church in all its richness) has been excellently presented in a concentrated form in Hans Küng's *On Being a Christian*,[4] where he describes trends among Catholics and Protestants: 'each ecclesia (= each individual assembly, congregation, Church) *is not the* ecclesia (= the universal Church, congregation, assembly), but fully *represents* the ecclesia'. 'It is only in the light of the local church and its concrete realisation that the universal Church can be understood.'

Free Churches sometimes have emphasised the independence of the local church in such a way that the universal Church has been lost sight of. This might have been due to the polemic situation in which many Free Churches have come into being, facing a national church with rather low priority given to the local church. Many Free Churches are rediscovering the universal Church. On the other hand, many churches, that have been predominantly concerned with the diocesan and the national church, are now discovering the local church.[5]

The discovery of the fundamental and inescapable interrelatedness between the local and the universal has not made it easier to find a simple answer to the problem of the authority in the Church.

4. AUTHORITY BY MEANS OF DIALOGUE

(*a*) Local *vis-à-vis* national/universal/ecumenical

(i) Authority in the Church must find expression in a way that pays attention to the

D

local church as well as to the universal Church. Authority grows out of a situation, where Christians (clergy and laity, women and men), conscious of their own faith, draw out its implications, with the experiences and insights of their daily life in mind, under the guidance of the Holy Spirit. These experiences are most concrete and specific in the life of the local congregation. Thus *the local congregation has a special authority*. But it must be balanced by the experiences of other congregations within the same denomination and within the wider Church.

(ii) Therefore, most Free Churches trust the authoritative wisdom of regional and national assemblies, speaking to local churches not by bureaucratic, legal systems but by means of advice and recommendations. In a world like ours, with all its plurality, with widely differing situations in different local situations within the same country and still wider differences between different parts of the world, in which the Church has to serve, it can be argued that *supreme authority must be with the local church, growing out of its unique experiences*.

(iii) But it can also be argued that in a world like ours the local church can be imprisoned in its own specificities, and that therefore national assemblies and international ecumenical councils and conferences have an *authority of outstanding importance*. This might be illustrated by the continuous, inward or outspoken dialogue going on year after year between members of local congregations of the Mission Covenant Church of Sweden, the local congregations themselves, on the one hand, and the World Council of Churches, on the other. Having shared the experiences of other member churches in the World Council of Churches, the Mission Covenant of Sweden feels it can speak with greater authority. And the authority of the World Council of Churches is fundamentally based upon the ongoing indirect dialogue even with local churches.

There is no easy way out of the tension between the local, the national, the ecumenical and the universal as to the problem of who has the say in the church. That tension is foreshadowed already in the New Testament (e.g., 1 Cor. 1:10; Acts 15).

(b) Laity—clergy

(i) In Free Church tradition ministers are considered important. A sign of that are all the theological seminaries they have established in many parts of the world for the training of ministers. Most Free Churches would agree to the statement: 'The essential and specific function of the special ministry is: *to assemble and build up the Christian community*, by proclaiming and teaching the Word of God, and presiding over the liturgical and sacramental life of the eucharistic community'.[6] Their authority might be disputed in the crisis of our time[7] but their rôle is of vital importance.

(ii) However, they are not the *esse* of the Church, only its *bene esse*. The Church needs them for its missionary task and for its own nurture, but they are not indispensable for the life of the Church. This has been illustrated in many countries, where for different reasons an ordained ministry has not been able or permitted to function.

According to Free Church tradition, the authority in the local congregation is not given to the ministers, the clergy, alone. *Basic* to almost all Free Churches is the idea of *the priesthood of all believers*, who might perform, if need be, all the ministerial functions mentioned above.[8] The priesthood of all believers is to be understood in a biblical way (1 Pet. 2:9), as a result of the Holy Spirit's equipment of all God's people for service in the world. It is not derived from modern democratic ideas, but it has had a dynamic democratic ferment in it (as is illustrated, e.g., by the remarkable rôle of the Free Churches in last century's democratic break-through in Sweden).

(iii) In the total life of the Church a *key role* is given *to the ordinary members*. They are not only responsible for the material welfare of the church (buildings, finances, etc.). They are the eyes, the ears and even the mouths of the church. It is by means of their experiences in professional, political, social, family and leisure life that much of that material is collected out of which grows the message of the Church. We hold the conviction, that even preaching grows out of Bible study in the light of this common experience of the local church.

(iv) The authority of the Church belongs to the whole Church, the whole *koinonia*, ministers and lay people together. This *koinonia* in Free Church tradition finds expression in the *local church meeting* or the national assembly, where every delegate from local churches has the right to speak. The outcome of that *koinonia* is an ethos, which gives direction and carries with it that authority, which might be expressed in public statements, sermons, editorials in church magazines, or in resolutions in controversial matters. According to Free Church tradition, the authority cannot be handed over to bishops or synods with legal power. *Authority is something that grows out of the common experiences of all members of the church, in the light of the Scripture and under the guidance of the Holy Spirit.* It might be a complicated and sometimes painful procedure. But only this authority, that grows out of this common, shared experience within the church carries weight and is sensitive enough to give guidance to women and men, young people and children within and outside the church.

(v) *Only by means of this continuous dialogue within the whole Church can real authority grow.* Only by means of this continuing dialogue within the Church, where the life experiences of all God's people are taken seriously can the Church live in and speak the truth of the gospel, in an era of radical changes in almost all areas of human existence.

Notes

1. A few words should be said about the church to which the author belongs, the Mission Covenant Church of Sweden, the largest free church in Sweden (the youth movement included); origin in last century's religious renewal in Sweden; mixed Lutheran-Reformed background, Congregational in character but with National Assembly with important functions (e.g., ordination of ministers, male and female, election of officers in the church); pietistic by tradition but culturally and politically active (three members of present Swedish Government members of the Mission Covenant); member of the World Council of Churches, the World Alliance of Reformed Churches/Presbyterian and Congregational and of the International Federation of Free Evangelical Churches.

2. Rather few systematic presentations of Free Church views are available. As to the Congregational tradition, see Daniel Jenkins *Congregationalism, A Restatement* (London 1960); *Proceedings of the Ninth International Congregational Council* (London 1962) and *Proceedings of the Tenth Assembly of the International Congregational Council* (London 1966); as to Baptist tradition, see Ernest A. Payne *The Fellowship of Believers*, Baptist Thought and Practice Yesterday and Today (London 1944).

3. See Norman Goodall in the 1962 Proceedings, mentioned above under note 2, James M. Gustafson (p. 33 ff. in the same Proceedings), and Jenkins (p. 70 ff.) in his book.

4. H. Küng 'The Pluriform Church' in *On Being a Christian* (New York 1978) esp. p. 478 ff.

5. See, e.g., the interesting analysis of this development in Jürgen Moltmann 'The Rediscovery of the Congregation' in *Hope for the Church* (Nashville 1979) p. 40.

6. *One Baptism, One Eucharist, and a Mutually Recognized Ministry*: Three Agreed Statements, World Council of Churches, Faith and Order paper No. 73 (Geneva 1975) p. 33.

7. About that crisis, see, e.g., H. Richard Niebuhr *The Purpose of the Church and Its Ministry* (New York 1956).

8. About stronger ministerial authority in Pentecostal churches, see Walter J. Hollenweger *Enthusiastisches Christentum* (Brockhaus 1969) p. 481.

Kurt Stalder

III. 6. An Old Catholic Response

(a) The Issue in Dispute

THE QUESTION of what must happen and what should in any case be done in order for the Church to remain in the truth has played a considerable rôle in its life from its earliest days. Even if the question as such does not come up for discussion, nevertheless every decision that is taken within the Church somehow or other implicitly involves this problem too. In addition the question has a special significance for Old Catholic theologians. It provided the setting for the dispute with the pope and for external separation from him. What was decided on by the majority at the First Vatican Council and proclaimed by the *papal dogma* of 1870 was meant to establish and determine how the Church should remain in the truth. But in the view of the Old Catholic fathers these decisions stood in opposition to scripture and tradition. This obliged them to resist. This resistance was in its turn answered by the pope with excommunication. And thus the Old Catholics saw themselves forced to build a Catholic Church while actually separated from the bishop of Rome.

What should not be overlooked is that not the least of the reasons for the intensity of the difference between the two sides is that both were pursuing *the same concern*: the preservation of the Church in the truth. *What was and is disputed* is *how this is to be achieved*. As far as the active elements in the Council majority were concerned the new dogmas provided the conclusive and only really satisfactory guarantee for the Church's being maintained in the truth. But the Old Catholic fathers were quite unable to discern how dogmas that in themselves represented innovations and thus a falling away from the truth could be able to serve the maintenance of the truth.

(b) Old Catholic Practice and Way of Life

The presupposition for everything that was done by Old Catholics in the context of this question thus consisted of the conviction that so far the Church had lived in the truth and that in consequence one simply had to reject all innovations and carry on doing what had been done previously. To this extent the idea of how the Church should be preserved in the truth appeared to the Old Catholic fathers less a problem than the requirement that it should not let itself be deflected from its original pattern of behaviour. In this way what was *contrasted with the dogmas of 1870 was not another idea*

42

but simply a way of life and a pattern of behaviour. Comprehensive and in some cases large-scale researches did admittedly bring together the evidence to show that the decisions of 1870 stood in contradiction to the Old Catholic tradition[1] and to indicate the developments that had led to a falling-away from the original pattern.

From these investigations and from the erection of the various dioceses and the documents and regulations that were needed to set them up the *elements* can be derived that are regarded as fundamental for the Church that wishes to remain in the truth. The most important elements are: frequent emphasis on the witness of scripture and the celebration of the Eucharist; the universal confession of faith of the early Church; the councils of the undivided Church and their decisions as an existing authority and a 'truly universal council' looked forward to as a future authority; the office of bishop, who is seen as bearing the chief responsibility for handing on and preserving the tradition of faith and its unity; the idea that all bishops with their Churches share the same mission; the restoration of the co-responsibility of the laity in the Churches.

The context and importance of these elements has been brought out more clearly by a process of further reflection necessitated both by experience and by the proliferation of ecumenical dialogue. Experience, for example, showed that granting the vote to the laity did not necessarily bring about their integration into the Church or that clinging to the confession of faith of the early Church did not guarantee that remaining in the faith would be something alive. This further reflection has also indicated the possibility of answering the question that forms the title of this essay, and this answer can now be set out under three heads.

2. ECCLESIOLOGY

(a) The Church as Community

The biblical authors may use different language to describe what took place in the mission, incarnation, death, resurrection and ascension of the son of God. They may conceive of it as an expiatory sacrifice, as a descent and ascent, or in other ways. But in any case what is involved is establishing community between God and us men and women and also community in God between us. If such community does not exist in the world, then one must say that the mission of God's son failed to reach its goal and has been without effect, that atonement and restoration do not exist.

If it does exist, however, it demonstrates the reality of the reconciliation and atonement that has taken place in Christ, it is itself the presence of everything that God has done in Christ. Where this community exists men and women are free with regard to God, to one another, to themselves: it is here that they have found their highest dignity, their partnership with God and the world, and therefore themselves. In God they have apprehended their independence, their autonomy. We believe that this community exists and that it is the Church. Where therefore this community that embraces heaven and earth exists, there is the Church. And where the Church is, there is this community that embraces heaven and earth. Hence we must say on the one hand that everywhere that the Church exists it is the one unique Church: there is only *one* Church. And on the other hand we must also say that *everywhere* that the Church exists it exists fully and not just a part of it, and to this extent there are many churches.

(b) The Mutual Responsibility of each church for the other churches in the one Church

No Church may regard itself or let itself be regarded as simply a part. Even if it is still very small or lives on the fringe of the world, it must not surrender anything of the dignity, freedom and independence which it has received through Christ and which it has to perfect and maintain in community with him. But at the same time it must not behave as if it were an isolated entity existing for itself alone. It must be open to all other churches, for visits, help, and dialogue, so that every church may be able to recognise and experience in every other the presence of the one and only Church. In this way every church shares responsibility for every other church.

The foundation of this community of the Church lies in the mission of Christ. It is he who has accepted us. Hence the Church exists only in the structure created by the relationship between Christ and ourselves. This structure is repeated in every relationship that can possibly exist in a Church. Fundamental to this is the complementary structure in which the relationship between Jesus and his disciples is reflected and confirmed, in other words the complementary structure of the bishop with the presbyterium on the one hand and the laity on the other. This complementary structure does not call the community into question but rather makes it possible. It is precisely in this complementary relationship that the two components are one: they are one inasmuch as they complement one another and each becomes the other's task and honour.

(c) The Apostolic Succession

It is in this complementary relationship that the apostolic or episcopal succession is situated or, to put it the other way round, this complementary relationship proceeds from the apostolic succession. In connection with this it should be noted that the term 'apostolic succession' is not understood in one of the erroneous ways that are often encountered. By this expression I mean the entire complex of patterns of behaviour and relationship by which the Church takes to itself all its tasks and duties and is thus aware of its responsibility for its existence.

This is expressed in its simplest form at the ordination of a bishop. A church has lost its bishop through death. Someone has already been elected to succeed him by the presbyterium and the laity. But however great the extent to which the church has itself chosen its new bishop it must equally be true that it does not bestow its bishop on itself but rather receives him. He is therefore ordained by another bishop and thus by the bishop of another church with the help of two co-consecrators who in their turn are bishops of other churches. This makes it clear that *every church is the Church one and entire and that for this reason every church and every bishop shares responsibility for every other church*. Those conducting the ordination examine and test the faith of the person they are ordaining and everyone, including the laity, professes the faith and mutually binds himself or herself to proclaim the gospel more widely and to do everything needed to build the Church up.

The following aspects are brought into particular prominence. If apostolic succession is to be understood in the way that has been set out above, and this is our opinion, then it follows that:

(i) the apostolic succession is the recognition of the *obligation of continuity* of persons and teaching with the apostles and with Christ and the realisation of this obligation, but not however an automatically effective mechanism of continuity;

(ii) because it is a continuity in the tasks given by Christ, it is also the *locus of the sacraments*, especially the Eucharist;

(iii) the realisation of apostolic succession provides the most solemn expression of the fact that *every church is the one Church*, that as a result every church and every bishop shares responsibility for every other bishop and his church, and that consequently the Church's unity and catholicity also contain the dimension of geographical universality; and

(iv) the continuity of apostolic succession is not simply a continuity of doctrine or of the sacrament, otherwise the Church would become merely an intellectual and authoritarian entity, but also a *continuity of persons* and this in their *complementary relationship of ministers and laity*. It is precisely apostolic succession by which the Church is constituted as a community for the seeking of awareness and commitment, a process in which all its members share and thereby discover their dignity and development.

With this presentation of the apostolic succession the decisive elements in considering the question how the Church can remain in the truth have in my opinion already been said. It is of course to be understood not in the sense of a recipe that can be applied mechanically with a guarantee of success, but in the sense of a promise: someone who is involved in the realisation of apostolic succession will also experience maintenance in the truth. It is the same as with proclamation: by preaching the gospel one cannot manufacture faith, but the person who does not listen will not learn that faith comes from preaching.

3. COUNCILS

Every statement of faith calls new questions into being, and these are answered in different ways on the basis of different experiences and points of view. The result quite soon is that, despite general basic agreement, there arise formulations with antithetical effects and in due course genuine differences. No one has ever succeeded in confining the dogmatic debate to past formulations that are highly regarded.[2] What happens in this case is that the processes of apostolic succession sketched out above lead not to the experience of agreement but to that of tensions and differences.

In this situation the fact that the entirety of the Church is present in every church and that every church ought to be able to recognise itself in every other and that they all thereby share responsibility for each other suggests that by means of their bishops they should come together to discuss matters: in brief, that they should come together for a small-scale or large-scale synod, perhaps for an ecumenical council. All the same even a council does not have the truth at its disposal. It is not therefore a suitable use of language to talk of a council deciding on a question of faith or of voting on it in the sense of a democratic assembly. Rather those taking part in the council can listen to each other and establish how things appear to everyone in the assembly. In this qualified majorities always turn out to be of particular pneumatological importance.[3] From this there emerges the council's confession of faith, in relation to which all members of all the churches have to take a stand during the process of reception.

4. THE DEEPEST GROUND FOR HOPE

The final sentences of the last two sections may appear rather naïvely optimistic. In view of Vatican I a somewhat more critical attitude might be expected from an Old Catholic theologian. But hope in the promise of the Spirit for the Church's remaining in the truth has in fact one more reason, discussion of which does not form part of our subject but would be of great importance. So far we have been talking about remaining in the truth to the extent that this is expressed in language. But the biblical view is that the truth is not identical with propositions. In the Bible the truth is the reality constituted by God the Father, Christ the Redeemer, and the Holy Spirit, the

Enlightener. There is no natural or automatic connection between words and the divine reality. Hence we understand each other only on the basis of a common experience of reality. Hence too *remaining in the truth is not exclusively dependent on verbal agreement in propositions*. Much more could be said about this, but it contains the ground *for hope*.

Translated by Robert Nowell

Notes

1. Especially characteristic is Joseph Langen *Geschichte der Römischen Kirche*, in four volumes (Bonn 1881-1893), and his *Das Vatikanische Dogma*, four parts in one volume (Bonn 1876). Significant, too, is J. H. Reinkens *Über die Einheit der katholischen Kirche* (Würzburg 1877). For the whole section on the historical aspect, see Urs Küry *Die Altkatholische Kirche* (Stuttgart ²1978).

2. H. J. Sieben *Die Konzilsidee der Alten Kirche* (Paderborn 1979) pp. 40 ff.

3. K. Stalder 'Autorität im Neuen Testament' in *Internationale Kirchliche Zeitschrift* (Stämpfli Berne) (1977) pp. 9 ff.

Leonardo Boff

IV. Matters requiring clarification

1. Is the distinction between *Ecclesia docens* and *Ecclesia discens* justified?

THIS IS a highly complex subject, and a complete treatment would really have to approach it sociologically, psychologically and ideologically, as well as theologically, to satisfy present-day critical requirements. This is because the distinction between one Church that speaks and teaches and another that listens and obeys, and the claim of a clerical body to be the guardians of truth, has led to violence and the practice of domination by some Christians over others. But the truth should set us free (John 8:32) and not oppress us; so, if we are to see the sense of the distinction despite its pathological practice by some sectors of the Church, we need to examine various aspects of the way in which such sense can be presented. But in the limited space available here, all I can do is put forward some theses relevant to the subject.

1. THE WHOLE CHURCH (THE *COMMUNITAS FIDELIUM*) MAKES UP THE *ECCLESIA DISCENS*

There is one God, one revelation, one liberating act by the Father in Christ through the Holy Spirit, one eternal life and one eschatology. The only responsible religious response to this saving event is that of faith. Faith is the human response to the *magnalia Dei*; it consists of saying, in the biblical sense, 'so be it', *Amen*, to the divine initiative. Faith requires silence, listening, attention. The Church is born of this response of faith; it consists of the community of those who give a res-ponse to God's pro-posal. So the whole Church is *Ecclesia discens*: student of the *unus Magister*, Jesus Christ (Matt. 23:8; and see 10:24; 13:13) and disciple of that Spirit of truth who will guide us into all truth (John 16:13), so that we have no need of anyone to teach us (1 John 2:27). If anyone in the Church (pope or bishop) did not first regard himself as a member of the Church *discens*, before any possible division of tasks within the Church, he would cease to be a sacramental member of the *communitas fidelium*, because he would have lost that substance that theologically constitutes the Church—faith. The distinction between *Ecclesia docens* and *Ecclesia discens* is only valid (assuming that it is) on condition that the *discens* side (the Church, hearer of the Word) is elevated above the *docens* side (the Church, witness to the saving events). We express the basic reason for this in the great doxology of the Mass, the Gloria: 'You alone are the Holy One, you alone are the Lord, you alone are the Most High, Jesus Christ'. This praise implies that 'you alone are the Teacher' and we are all the disciples who still hear the call to 'come, follow me' (Mark 10:21). The Spirit still continues to 'declare to us the things that are to come' (John 16:13) and to teach us all things (14:26).

2. THE WHOLE CHURCH (THE *COMMUNITAS FIDELIUM*) MAKES UP THE *ECCLESIA DOCENS*

The primary task of the community of faith is to enable others too to say 'so be it', *Amen*, to God. This is the mission to make others disciples (Matt. 28:19). Peter's first sermon in Acts shows the teaching practice of those who listened to and accepted the saving acts of God: 'Give ear to my words . . . hear these words. . . . This Jesus God raised up and of this we are all witnesses' (Acts 2:14, 22, 32). Faith speaks and witnesses after being heard and accepted. It speaks so that others too 'may have fellowship with us' (1 John 1:3), and come to swell the ranks of those who believe. Through faith expressed in baptism, all are drawn into the mystery of Christ and made bearers of the Spirit (see Rom. 8:9, 23; 1 Cor. 3:16, 19), all are sent forth to bear witness. Therefore all make up the *Ecclesia docens*, teaching the rest of humanity what good things God has done for them all.

3. *DOCENS* AND *DISCENS* ARE TWO FUNCTIONS, NOT FRACTIONS, OF THE CHURCH

In the community born of faith there is a time to listen and a time to speak, a time to learn from revelation and a time to witness to revelation. *Docens* and *discens* are two determinants of the same, sole community; they are two adjectives which qualify two functions of the whole community; they are not two nouns which introduce a dichotomy in the community. To be both teacher and learner emerges as a dual function of one and the same Church and not as two fractions of the Church or within the Church.

There is a mutual apprenticeship in the Church: there is a moment when the hierarchy should listen, study the Scriptures, pay attention to the signs of the times, hear the cry of the poor reaching up to heaven and discern what God's will for all mankind is; there is a moment when lay people must speak and witness to the truth of the gospel applied to the social situation in which they live, even when this leads to the blessedness of being persecuted. In these moments the hierarchy feel themselves members of the learning Church, and lay people feel themselves members of the teaching Church. Each is master and pupil of the other and all are followers of the gospel. This co-existence and simultaneity of the two functions should bring us to heed Jesus' appeal for no one to be called master, father or spiritual director, since we are all brothers and sisters of one another (see Matt. 23:8-10).

4. THE CONDITIONS OF A DISTINCTION BETWEEN TEACHING AND LEARNING CHURCH

The distinction between Ecclesia docens *and* Ecclesia discens *is theologically valid only once socio-analytical reflection on religious division of labour has been assumed and surpassed.*

(a) The conditions of a special teaching office

Despite the basic equality of all in the Church, since all are brethren and disciples, despite the simultaneity of the two functions, there is still an office in the Church *which* takes on the function of teaching in a special way. This is not now concerned with witnessing and teaching in the general sense, but in the particular sense, technically as it were, in an official and authentic form. We are dealing now with the *power* of teaching, which the pope and the bishops feel has been given particularly to them. And together with this power goes a hierarchy of power. How did this specialisation come about?

The theology of the manuals, particularly those of canon law, states that the Church of Christ is essentially hierarchical by divine ordinance. As Salaverri says: 'This means that there exists in it, through the will of its divine founder, a discrimination by which certain persons have to be called to exercise the essential powers, to the exclusion of the rest, by a law established by Christ himself'.[1] Christ, it is argued, is the Messiah-master, to whom all power has been given; he transmitted this power to the apostles (Matt. 28:18-20) in such a way that 'he who hears you hears me, and he who rejects you rejects me' (see Luke 10:16). We are here faced with an epiphanic vision of the Church, in which it would have emerged completely structured from the will of its founder.

It should be remarked that this interpretation is based on a literal reading of the texts as they have been handed down, without considering the stages through which they might have passed or the theologies reflected in their different layers. Furthermore, those who make these statements are those who benefit from them (the hierarchy); from a critical point of view, a speech by the protagonist of the action must be regarded as ideological. So in order to guarantee the validity of an authentic *magisterium* we must go beyond an epiphanic view of the early development of the Church and look for a theological concept capable of taking account of all the aspects present in the affirmation of faith: Jesus founded a Church.

In the first place, such a theology must take account of the historical-critical findings of exegesis. These tell us that the Church cannot in any way be placed at the centre of Jesus' main concerns; any authentic sayings relating to the structuring of a community are extremely few and far between.[2] This does not mean that it is meaningless to speak of Christ as the foundation of the Church, but neither is it right to be ingenuous and disregard the findings of exegesis.

(b) Teaching and learning: an unoppressive division of labour

In the second place, socio-religious knowledge of the growth of hierarchies[3] and *religious division of labour*,[4] also has to be taken into consideration. The great religions, including Christianity, are associated with the growth of cities, which introduced a separation between city and country and the first social division of labour into manual and intellectual. It was Max Weber who first showed how urbanisation contributed to the 'rationalisation' of religion, through the formation of a body of experts responsible for preserving and interpreting, officially and authentically, the religious capital common to all the faithful. So there arose an *Ecclesia docens* and an *Ecclesia discens*. As Bourdieu has written: 'The clerical body is a direct consequence of the rationalisation of religion and derives the principles of its legitimacy from a theology raised to the status of dogma whose validity and perpetuation it ensures'.[5] So from the bosom of a community of equals there emerged a hierarchy for a few and a diaconate for the rest.

From a modern standpoint, any theological reflection which fails to take account of these facts runs the risk of exercising an objectively ideological function and of mystifying aspects which can be explained by historically identifiable causes. In other words, even if Christ had said nothing about the power of teaching authentically there would still be such a magisterial office in the Church. Theologically this means that Christ's will to found a Church does not dispense from, but includes the normal means by which a religious community guarantees fidelity to its original identity through a body of experts in communion with all the faithful. Emile Durkheim has shown that division of labour does not necessarily lead to substantivising of functions, but can maintain an internal solidarity with a common base,[6] providing a useful and necessary function of preserving, amplifying and clarifying. In this form the distinction between the Church *docens* and *discens* is justifiable, since it remains a function of the community of brethren. It is a *distinction within the community, not an institution outside and above it.*

St Matthew expresses this dialectic well: on the one hand the power to bind and loose resides in the whole community (18:18); on the other, it resides particularly in the principle of unity of the community, i.e., in Peter (16:19). Early ecclesiology taught that the *potestas sacra* was given *generaliter* to the Church (*communitas fidelium*) and *specialiter* to the bishops and presbyters.[7] The bearer subject is nonetheless the community, from within which the magisterial function emerges as its organ of expression.

5. DIVISIVE UNDERSTANDING OF THE CHURCH *DOCENS* AND *DISCENS* STEMS FROM A PATHOLOGICAL VIEW OF THE REALITY OF THE CHURCH

Any healthy organism can, historically, have its pathological aspects. This has happened with this subject. There were times, particularly after the Gregorian reforms, when the Church was above all the clergy. On the basis of this fact, the *Ecclesia docens* has tended to form a sociological state apart from the rest. The setting-up of a body of experts set apart from the community was accompanied by a process of effective expropriation of the religious power of the other members of the community, who became 'merely' lay people, deprived of the productive force of symbolic goods and reduced to simple spectators of the life of the Church. This rigid separation between clergy and laity was reinforced by Gregory XVI (1831-46): 'No one can doubt that the Church is an unequal society, in which God has destined some to rule and some to serve. The latter are the laity and the former the clergy'. Pius X went still further: 'Only the college of pastors has the right and the authority to direct and govern. The masses have no rights at all except to let themselves be governed like the obedient flock following its shepherd'.[8]

Paulo Freire has shown the pathological nature of this type of relationship which dehumanises one side and the other.[9] On one side is the *Ecclesia docens*, which knows everything and interprets everything; on the other the laity who know nothing, produce nothing and receive everything, the *Ecclesia discens*. The hierarchy learns nothing from contact with these lay people; they in their turn have no ecclesial space in which to demonstrate their riches. This denies the ontological vocation of every human being and every Christian in particular, which is to be a participant in and not merely a spectator of the history of salvation. In this pathological situation, religious education fails to liberate one side or the other and is dehumanising.

Vatican II—not before time—redressed the balance, restoring threatened theological sanity. The Church is basically the people of God; all share in the teaching office of Christ, including the laity (LG § 35); within this people, the hierarchy has an official office, but always one of service to the whole Christian community (LG § 25).

6. DIALECTICAL INTERACTION AS A HEALTHY DISTINCTION BETWEEN *ECCLESIA DOCENS* AND *ECCLESIA DISCENS*

If it is to be legitimate and respect its evangelical purpose, all power must know its own limits. Otherwise it falls into the temptation of all power groups, which is to absolutise themselves. This means purely and simply to oppress all those outside. In the history of the Church, the articulation of the two poles of *docens* and *discens* almost always in favour of the former (the hierarchy) has led to situations which are unacceptable in the light of gospel criteria (Luke 22:25-28). The way was a single track going from the hierarchy who taught to the people who hardly heard. We need a two-track way, from the learners to the teachers as well as from the teachers to the learners. If this is to work, we need to observe the following rules:

(*a*) *open dialogue on both sides:* All must listen, especially those who have to speak authentically (the hierarchy), and all must have guaranteed room in which to speak; there must be an exchange of knowledge, with no one trying to dominate another, but always being attentive to others because the Spirit is in everyone;

(*b*) *an attitude of mutual criticism* as a way of preventing absolutisation and domination, and as 'the only way in which people can realise their natural vocation to integration, overcoming the attitude of adjustment or accommodation',[10] seeing in the signs of the times a specific message for the Church; and

(*c*) *a point of reference 'outside ourselves':* The Church does not exist for its own sake but for that of the world which must be evangelised and saved. Both the teaching and the learning Church should always keep the world as a point of reference—and the Spirit, who embraces the world as well as the Church. It is in this vertical and horizontal interaction that a healthy and valid relationship between authentic speaking and obedient listening can be guaranteed within one and the same Church.

Translated by Paul Burns

Notes

1. S. Salaverri 'La potestad de Magisterio Eclesiástico y asintimiento que le es debido' *Estudios Eclesiásticos* 29 (1955) 155-195; *idem, Sacra Theologicae Summa* I 3 'De Ecclesia' (1952) nn. 117-141.

2. See L. Boff *Eglise en genèse* (Paris 1978) pp. 64-88; H. Küng *The Church* (London and New York 1968) pp. 54-79.

3. See H. Dombois *Hierarchie: Grund und Genze einer umstritenen Struktur* (Freiburg 1981) esp. pp. 11-22.

4. See M. Weber *Wirtschaft und Gesellschaft* (Cologne-Berlin 1964) I pp. 124 ff., 688 ff.; P. Bourdieu 'Genèse et structure du champ religieux' *Rev. Fr. de Sociologie* 12 (1971) 295-334.

5. *A economia das trocas simbólicas* (São Paulo 1974) p. 38.

6. *De la division du travail social.*

7. See Y.-M. Congar *L'Ecclésiologie du haut Moyen-Age* (Paris 1968) esp. pp. 92-98.

8. See M. Schmaus *Der Glaube der Kirche* II (Munich 1970) p. 102.

9. *Pedagogy of the Oppressed* and *Education as Practice of Liberation.*

10. *Ibid.*

Gabriel Daly

IV. 2. Which *Magisterium* is authentic?

THE LITERATE Christian imagination is haunted by Dostoyevsky's story, 'The Grand Inquisitor'. In that story two embodiments of religious authority face each other on a summer's night in a dungeon of the Inquisition in sixteenth-century Seville. The Inquisitor's claim to authenticity derives partly from the cynical pragmatism of his political analysis but mainly from the jurisdiction and political power attaching to his office. The prisoner's authenticity (he does not need to claim it) derives from his person, his words, his acts, and, above all, from his deep and delicate concern for freedom in the response of those who meet him. For all its hyperbole, the story stands as an answer in parable form to the question assigned to me in this short essay.

I shall not be concerned here with the juridical senses of the word 'authentic' and therefore with such problems as the respective rights of popes, bishops, and councils. In fact I would wish to argue that, important as these institutional questions may be in themselves, they are controlled by the conception one has of what it means to *teach*, especially to teach religious and moral truths and values.

1. THE AUTHORITARIAN AND THE DIALOGICAL MODELS OF TEACHING

The term 'magisterium' is a neologism which achieved general currency in the Catholic Church during the nineteenth century, when the common model of *all* teaching, secular as well as religious, was one of an authoritarian imparting of information. The teacher occupied a position of eminence from which he dictated to his pupils (often literally). At the opposite pole from this conception lies the 'Socratic' method whereby the teacher seeks through question and dialogue to elicit an authentic personal and internal response from his pupils.

A great deal of *twentieth-century educational reform* has consisted in attempts to have this method more widely recognised and practised. This reform was reflected in the catechetical renaissance in primary and secondary religious education which flourished in the 1960s. It has of course also percolated into third-level theological teaching. The one area from which it is still too often absent is the official *magisterium* of the Roman Catholic Church for which the model of teaching remains that of an authoritarian body concerned with the provision of 'correct' information about Catholic beliefs and practices.

Since the Church as a body has been charged with the task of teaching, it is surely not unreasonable to expect that its members at every institutional level, even the highest, will seek to employ methods and techniques which are in keeping both with the gospel and with the best educational insights of the age. It does a serious disservice to the Word of God to imprison it in educational philosophies and techniques which belong to a bygone age and which may now actually be *experienced as alienating*. If the prevailing conception of what is involved in the teaching process is an inherently alienating one, there is no point in posing a question about authenticity. An alienating medium results in a distorted message, especially in matters of religious truth and moral instruction.

As Christians we are committed to the conviction that the truth we profess is the truth which sets men and women free. Such truth can never be authentically professed on purely extrinsic grounds, because the freedom it engenders is *ab initio* an interior one. This kind of *truth demands an unforced and unfeigned inner assent which cannot be produced by any purely extrinsic authority*. Extrinsicism of the kind which dominated official Catholic theology in the period between the two Vatican councils is the very seed-bed of inauthenticity. It had been ably criticised by Maurice Blondel and Lucien Laberthonnière during the modernist crisis, but the ruthless and indiscriminate condemnations of 1907 ensured that it would hold sway until the Church in council disposed of it in the 1960s.

The conception of the *magisterium* which prevailed from the Munich Brief (1863) down to the meeting of the Second Vatican Council was the product of a theology which that council implicitly abandoned as a mandatory expression of Catholic belief. In the heady age which followed on Vatican II Roman Catholic theologians have been engaged in the challenging and disturbing business of exploring all the implications of the council's break with mandatory scholasticism. The council offered little guidance on how to live with the new pluralism which it had itself brought about; nor had it much to say about the freedom of theological inquiry. It gave Catholic theology a new lease of life without a charter for institutional security in the living of it. It enabled Catholic theologians to join with their Protestant colleagues in the perennial task of exploring their beliefs with a view to influencing and being influenced by critical and scientific developments since the Enlightenment; but it gave them no guarantee that there would be no return to pre-conciliar attitudes on the part of the Church's government.

2. THEOLOGICAL AUTHENTICITY AND THE FREEDOM OF THEOLOGY

Thus under the direct stimulus of the council the search for theological authenticity began in earnest, much to the dismay of those Catholics for whom radical uniformity under strictly centralised authority was an essential ingredient of their Catholicity. Others who supported the initial reforms with enthusiasm appear to have lost their nerve when they realised that the search for authenticity has an inner logic of its own which resists the panic cry 'thus far and no farther'.

The quest for truth necessarily implies the shock of the unfamiliar and the risk of short-term error. It therefore remained to be seen whether those who exercise the highest kinds of institutional authority in the Church would be able and willing to trust the processes of *free expression* and *free debate* in the knowledge that theological positions normally generate spontaneous and autonomous dialectical correctives (as Protestant theology has so often shown). The 'Socratic' method needs time and space to work itself through any situation. Conscious acquiescence in partial authenticity as a final goal is not a morally defensible option. Herein lies the origin of much of today's tension between free theological inquiry and an official *magisterium* which continues to see itself not merely as the final arbiter of Catholic orthodoxy but also apparently as its initiator and its judge of first instance. (The medieval universities enjoyed a freedom of inquiry and debate which was denied to Catholic theologians in the period between the two Vatican councils.)

Orthodoxy and authenticity are unfortunately not synonymous. Orthodoxy is the result of a *process* which needs time and space to run its course. If the process is prematurely interfered with, the result will be an inauthentic 'orthodoxy' which is little more than ideological verbalising.

3. TEACHING OFFICE AND THEOLOGY

A theologian who writes a book which explores an old question in a new way should not be thought of as 'teaching' in the old-fashioned 'magisterial' sense of transmitting authorised instruction. This is one reason why, in my view, theologians should firmly reject any suggestion that they are exercising any kind of 'magisterium', 'parallel', or even 'subordinate'. If they think of themselves as teachers, it should always be in the 'Socratic' sense of raising questions, advancing hypotheses, and criticising the arguments of others, thereby, in the poet Robert Browning's expressive phrase, 'lending their minds out'. It is this lending out of their minds, with all its professional—not to mention institutional—risks, which constitutes their particular service in and to the Church.

For much of the Church's history the papal or conciliar *magisterium* was exercised usually at the end of a long debating process, and then only if the faith and peace of the Church were seen to be in obvious jeopardy. Today it has become normal for the official *magisterium* to issue *teaching documents* spontaneously, as it were. Unless these documents are regarded as material for continuing and open discussion (and there is rarely any indication that this is how their authors see them), a thoroughly inauthentic situation can result. Since they normally invoke evidence and employ argumentation, they *are theological documents* and as such *open to examination and criticism*. In the nature of the case they will normally bear the hallmarks of one particular school of theology. If they are put forward as 'the teaching of the Church', and therefore as having at least a provisional claim upon the believer's faith and obedience, they may create a gratuitous conflict in the minds and hearts of loyal Catholics. Since *arguments are of themselves conclusive or non-conclusive, they cannot be imposed by extrinsic authority*.

The relationship between faith and its theological articulation constitutes a difficult and sensitive problem. The Church has been given the explicit task of proclaiming a faith which is true to its origins and primal inspiration. It has also been given the implicit task of seeing that faith is explored anew in every age, so that it may speak authentically to every age.

To concentrate on the first task to the detriment of the second can betray the gospel message by placing it in an increasingly obsolescent museum surrounded by armed guards. This was in effect what happened to Catholic theology in the period which followed the Enlightenment. Little or no significant field-work was done. New insights and techniques were ignored and often condemned. The museum was run, not for the public good, but for the comfort and security of its custodians. It conserved its magnificent treasures from the past but only at the cost of sacrificing the present and future. The Second Vatican Council dismissed the armed guard and commissioned new field-work. The custodians of the museum had no alternative but to go along with the new programme. That field-work lacks the comfort and security of museum activities, but it contributes greatly to the authentic display of the Church's treasures. A *magisterium* which recognised and actively promoted this field-work would indeed be seen to be caring for truth and authenticity. A museum which was more concerned with the authority of its custodians than with the treasures committed to its care would be rightly accused of narcissistic administration and misplaced values. A *magisterium* which seemed to be obsessed with its own authority would be drawing attention away from the message and focussing it on the medium. Only in Christ are the medium and the message identical.

4. AUTHENTICITY MEANS HAVING THE MIND OF CHRIST

The Church derives its authority, its credentials and its mission from Christ. Thus in the *juridical* sense it can be rightly said to derive its authenticity from Christ. *Authenticity* in its primary sense, however, *is a matter of having the mind of Christ*, with Christ's delicate sensitivity to the unfeigned response of others to his teaching and initiatives. A Church which was constantly proclaiming and defending its authority and authority-structures could be reasonably suspected of having lost confidence in the inner power of its message. It would also be setting up a counter-witness to that message, for it would simply confirm onlookers in the suspicion that they were watching, not a shared exercise in the discernment of truth, but a raw struggle for power.

The Inquisitor recognised the point at issue when he said to his prisoner: 'Instead of taking possession of men's freedom you multiplied it and burdened the spiritual kingdom of man with its sufferings for ever. You wanted man's free love so that he should follow you freely, fascinated and captivated by you.' An authentic *magisterium* is one which resists the ever-present temptation to take possession of men's freedom but which instead is ready to trust the intrinsic truth of the message committed to its care, ready also to trust the faithful, if sinful, men and women who are wrestling with its meaning and implications for a world which has lost its way but which will certainly not be inspired to return again to the search by anachronistic demonstrations of inquisitorial power.

E

Luigi Sartori

IV. 3. What is the Criterion for the *Sensus Fidelium*?

THE PROBLEM of the 'sensus fidelium' is, I feel, entering a new phase. Vatican II had already marked one stage; henceforth it was no longer possible, as had been done after Vatican I, to make a distinction between the *teaching* Church and the *learning* Church, between an *active* subject on the one hand and a *passive* subject on the other, almost as though the pastors were not themselves in fact believers, and almost as though the *magisterium* were 'superior to faith and has at its disposal the full knowledge of truth' (I am quoting here word for word from a statement by the Polish episcopate at the Council regarding the controversial Section 12 of *Lumen Gentium* on the 'sensus fidei').[1] Section 12 of *Lumen Gentium* attributes solely to the Holy Spirit a direct causality ('excitatur et sustentatur') in the arousal of the sense of faith, while acknowledging to the *magisterium* merely a guiding function ('sub ductu').

But at the 1980 Synod of Bishops (dedicated to the family) I think a step forward was taken. The method of 'seeing, judging, acting' (adopted by the YCW, contained in *Gaudium et Spes* and common in almost all the post-conciliar pastoral texts and projects) has increasingly urged the question of whether the first phase, that of *recognising the situation (seeing), represents merely a collection of data, or whether it can be interpreted as an authentic search for the 'sensus fidelium'*? At the 1980 Synod, in the very first phase devoted to reporting on the various attitudes existing at grass-roots level in the Church (where the problem was also included of the low level of compliance with official moral doctrine, and thus also with *Humanae Vitae*), one synodal Father boldly appealed to the 'sensus fidelium'.[2] Others contested the legitimacy of such an appeal; and they called up again the shade of a past dominated by that Manichaean *a priori* which dictates suspicion of the actions at the grass roots from the outset and attribution of any distancing or deviation from the official position is detected, to the workings of the 'evil spirit' and not the Holy Spirit!

However, the problem today is not situated at the level of theoretical principles, but at the level of *verification and concrete application*. Indeed the discussion on *criteria* must *above all* bear on concrete living conditions in order to create a Church capable of producing a valid *sensus fidei*. The prophet comes before the prophecy; we lack prophecy because we lack prophets; the criteria of discernment of an authentically prophetic Church come primarily from the criteria of discernment of prophecy.[3]

1. FOR A CHURCH WHICH GIVES SCOPE TO THE 'SENSUS FIDELIUM'

Two types of conditioning can be distinguished: those relating to fidelity to the divine, or to the Word and the Spirit, and those relating to fidelity to the human, or to history.

(a) Criteria relating to the divine

The criteria relating to the 'divine' are summed up in the main themes of the ecclesiology of communion, ratified by Vatican II. From the theoretical point of view these themes are being confirmed constantly, so that to recall them here yet again would be a boring exercise. May we therefore just briefly sketch out the main points which most directly touch on our theme.[4]

(i) *Faith is the radical 'primum' in the Church;* it is that in which we are all equal, brothers, all and always *believers*, held to 'obedience of the faith', to submission to the Word, all in need of receiving instruction and training. Prospective *fathers* and *teachers* can be such only in this way, and this is certainly not to hinder or diminish, but rather to accentuate the equality and brotherhood which unite them to other believers.

(ii) Similarly, *all are equipped by the Spirit*, and by its gifts, to *give* to others, and rendered capable of *teaching* their brothers. The Church places itself at the service of the 'pleroma', of the fullness of Christ, to the degree in which it makes manifest the apparition of the eschatological era, or of the era of gathering up the charisms poured forth by the Spirit. Not even a 'fragment' may be lost (see John 6:12).

(iii) The gifts of the Spirit, including faith, are not concerned with the static and abstract contemplation of doctrine, but with the *history and dynamism of the development* of the *implications* of the seed of the Word, to bring its fruits to maturity, whether at the level of cognitive insight or at that of verification through practical experience. The 'sensus fidei' of Section 12 of *Lumen Gentium* is a gift which allows one to 'penetrate [the faith] more deeply by accurate insights' (*the poetic aspect*) and to 'apply it more thoroughly to life' (the practical aspect). Faith, however, is a gift of the capacity to plan, to progress, to anticipate the future.

(iv) The ideal form of this progress is consent: unanimity, although in the diversity of historical expressions. The 'consensus of believers' is a final criterion, an ultimate goal, in comparison with which the 'consensus of teachers' is a criterion which is merely functional, a guarantee and historical instrument which, however, should also appear to be temporary.

(b) The criteria relating to the 'human'

The criteria relating to the 'human' concern that which today, perhaps, to a greater extent conditions the Church in its capacity to produce a *sensus fidei*, to make itself prophetic. The *humanisation of the Church*, in an incarnate form, is a necessary condition for its divine element (its being 'people of God', its faith as 'project of salvific history') to be manifest, and to be at least meaningful for the world. *Gaudium et Spes* urges such fidelity to man, to the values which can be garnered from experience and history (Section 44). In this sector too we shall limit ourselves to pointing out briefly the main appeals to concreteness made to us by today's culture.

(i) The anthropological sciences insist on *communication before communion*. Without true communication communion does not occur. The *sensus fidei* cannot flourish in a Church where the consensus is expressed as mechanical repetition by an anonymous crowd; only free persons who freely communicate with one another can realise true consensus.

From this point of view it becomes absolutely necessary to take note of reactions, feedback: a true realisation of communication must be grasped on the basis of the 'receivers' and on the degree with which the latter 'react'. The classic theological thesis of 'receptio' requires, therefore, to be broadened and deepened. The *active reaction of believers (whether in consensus or in dissent) can in fact be described as a true locus theologicus*, in which it is possible to read the force of the transmitted Word, to grasp its original resonances and ever new implications.[5] It is in this context that discussion on public opinion in the Church, already officially taken up by the Church in *Communio et Progressio* of 1974 (Sections 114-121) can come alive.

(ii) Being realistic about communication means *accepting the element of conflict* as a quite normal *de facto* situation. We would therefore do well not to extol consensus *a priori* and acritically, nor to suspect and be distrustful of dissent *a priori*; in concrete terms, either one can be a normally ambiguous phenomenon, which conceals pathological or at least immature realities.[6]

(iii) The ambiguity which easily contaminates both dissent and consensus involves making of consensus a *problem not so much—nor immediately—one of 'number' but rather one of quality*. It has always been tried, in the history of the Church, to single out the so-called 'sanior pars' in order to find out the 'vox populi'.[7] But today we are encouraged and trained to suspect the presence of 'deforming' elements even within the exercise of the rôle of teachers: the ideological character, or the supportive or protective function of certain political choices, does not sway merely some sector or other of the teachings proposed by the experts, nor just what the grass-roots are saying. On the other hand the affirmation of a 'sense of belonging' which is only partial (and with a wide range of forms and degrees) is no longer a rare phenomenon or one of merely minor importance; statistics now prove it to be a normal or at least quite a common fact.[8] And so it is no longer either possible or permissible to appeal to the 'sense of the believers' too hastily and too innocently!

(iv) There is more and more scope, however, for *the historical dialectic of trends, for a sort of alternation of majorities*. Unanimity constitutes only a remote, ideal goal; it is becoming more and more necessary to accept that we have to reckon with simple majorities. Orthodoxy, in this light, would appear to be a necessary integration of alternately winning theses, where each successive victory brings about a recuperation of aspects of the truth of theses which were formerly the losers. Truth is situated beyond and above victories and defeats, because any victory as a rule contains within itself an incapacity to evaluate every aspect, at least those concealed in the losing thesis.[9] Here again we have a verification of the principle according to which history is moved by the leaven of the predecessors, by the intentions and aspirations of the losers and the defeated.

(v) Finally, I wish to discuss here the *true nature of the ecumenical style*. Ecumenism cannot mean 'psychological or sociological removal of conflicts'. Ecumenical consensus cannot be synonymous with artificial peace, still less with concealment of differences.[10] *Antitheses* become *authentic complements* only when they are placed within a Whole and in a Catholicity which gives real scope to personal and group identity, to a clear identification of the problems, to frank and sincere discussion of opinions, to the widest possible variety of choices.

2. FOR A DISCERNMENT OF THE *SENSUS FIDELIUM*

The conditions so far examined already represent criteria, if only remote, for the discernment of the *sensus fidelium*. In our opinion, however, they are the more decisive ones, even on the basis of the premises alone: rather the prophet than the prophecy, rather a Church capable of entertaining and generating a *sensus fidei* than the *sensus fidei* in itself. But now a few words on this second matter.

(*a*) Discussion usually bears by preference on *limits*, and in particular on *objective* limits: the *sensus fidei* is competent, it is said, only in easy, common, universal questions; not, however, in subtle and complicated ones. This is true. But something should be added straight away: today the medium of cultural information has developed; critical capacity is spreading more and more; theological education is at times becoming a mass fact; the opinions of 'the people' could therefore also touch on the 'highest' questions, at least indirectly and negatively.

(*b*) Another favourite limit for circumscribing the value of the sense of believers is *practice*. Practical behaviour seems to constitute the most suitable field for the competence of the *sensus fidelium*. But here too definitions should be made analogous to those indicated above: 'practice' is never without incidence on 'theory'; verification is itself one path of exploration and investigation of truth (and not of one application only), especially if the ideological character which accompanies a large part of our theological activities is taken into account.

(*c*) The problem of representativity is also becoming more and more exacting; in fact, in deciphering the 'feelings of the people' one is constrained to resort to go-betweens, at least as regards the interpretation of the data collected in inquiries or any generalised summing up of 'what people are thinking'. In this area, appeal is too often and to the point of abuse made to the 'silent majority'; the 'silence of the others' is used as an instrument and the weight constituted by the numbers of the absent is wielded as a force.[11]

In this connection it is urgently necessary to bear in mind the evangelical criterion of *solidarity with the last*, and above all with sinners and outlaws, on the model of Jesus, who identified himself above all with outcasts. An ecclesiastical system which, in order to ascertain the 'sense of the faithful' or public opinion in the Church, in fact favours those who already have power, in order to make of it a question of further power, could not equip a Church capable of listening and truly understanding 'what the Spirit says to the churches' (see Rev. 2:7).

CONCLUSION

The *sensus fidelium* does constitute a more and more decisive and inevitable 'theological place'; but it is more difficult too, because it is complex and easily manipulable. Some however favour other 'places', those which offer greater securities, which are 'juridically authentic'; it is convenient then to justify oneself by citing the 'juridical incompetence' of the people, and therefore the need for authoritative mediation. Others, on the other hand, refer, wherever convenient, to the numerical weight of that elusive silent majority, in order in this way to rid themselves of the bother of listening, of allowing an opinion, and of interpreting only after having listened.

The evangelical ideal remains, however, that all have a voice, actively, in the Church. As Moses said: 'Would that all the Lord's people were prophets!' (Num. 11:29); and Paul said: 'For you can all prophesy one by one, so that all may learn and all be encouraged' (1 Cor. 14:31).

Translated by Della Couling

Notes

1. See *Acta Synodalia Sacrosancti Concilii Eocumenici Vaticani II* (Rome 1971) II, Pars I, pp. 600-601.

2. See the Report by Cardinal Ratzinger in *Osservatore Romano* of 8 October, p. 2: 'The criterion of doctrine must be the sense of faith of the people of God, the experience of spouses . . .'.

3. See *Spirito Santo e Storia* ed. L. Sartori (Rome 1977) pp. 36-37: 'The prime criteria of discernment of the Spirit are those which decide the true way of putting oneself in a "prophetic" situation, of competence for "munus propheticum". Prophecy comes after the prophet'.

4. Specific bibliographical data on the subject of 'sensus fidelium' can be found in Y. Congar *La Tradizione e le tradizioni*, I (esp. pp. 367-383, with reference in particular to Newman's 'illative sense') and II (esp. pp. 154-179) (Rome 1964-65); *idem*, 'Reception as on Ecclesiological Reality' *Concilium* 77 (1972) 43-68; there are also good bibliographies in P. Granfield 'The *Sensus Fidelium* in Episcopal Selection' in *Concilium* 137 (1980) 33-38.

5. See L. Sartori 'Resconto sul XXI Convegno Teologico Triveneto su "Teologia e Psicologia"' in *Studia Patavina* 1 (1974) 248-255.

6. *Ibid.*, p. 251: 'Consensus and dissent easily become, at the unconscious level, symptoms of frustration, of conflict, of a need for compensation and security, even though this is less frequent and less probable in dissent than in consensus; at the conscious level, however, dissent more easily expresses a greater thrust toward creativity, although it might involve suffering' (*N.B.*, here the tools of psychology are being applied to the problem of 'consensus and dissent within the Church').

7. See B. Schimmelpfennig 'The Principle of the *Sanior Pars* in the Election of Bishops during the Middle Ages' in *Concilium* 137 (1980) 16-23.

8. See the 'Resoconto' (report) cited in Note 5: with regard to the 'sense of belonging' psychology poses the problem of its continuity in time, and points out the Church's commitment to 'return to the models of the origins, to the search for intermediate microstructures, to the valorisation of basic groups and communities', and illustrates how 'the diversity of intensity in the sense of belonging allows only partial identifications with the Church' (*ibid.*, p. 253).

9. See C. Gerest 'Nostalgia dell' unità nella Chiesa e politica di soffocamento dei conflitti' in *Concilium* 9 (1975) 56-76 (this is one of a number of articles which were not printed in the English language edition between 1974-1976: Language editor's note).

10. *Ibid.* pp. 72-74.

11. See J. Ratzinger *Dizionario Teologico*, ed. H. Fries, III (Brescia 1968) *sub. nom.* 'Reppresentanza', pp. 42-53.

Avery Dulles

Successio apostolorum—
Successio prophetarum—
Successio doctorum

THE TERM 'succession' (*diadochē*) may be understood as expressing an essential attribute of the Church—its permanence within change. Succeeding to Christ, the Church renders him visibly present in continually changing situations. Jesus himself, as Lord of the Church, is in a unique and pre-eminent sense, God's apostle (*apostolos*, Heb. 3:1), prophet (*prophētēs*, Matt. 21:11, etc.) and teacher (*didaskalos*, Matt. 8:19, etc.). Hence it is not surprising that the Church, which represents him, should have, among other functions, these three. Commissioned by the Lord, it is his apostle. Filled with his Spirit, it is sent as a prophet and teacher to the nations.

In the body of Christ, there is a certain division of labour. Some members specialise in some functions, others in others. Among the diverse specialisations Paul singles out for particular attention 'first apostles, second prophets, third teachers' (1 Cor. 12:28). Each of these three primary forms of service is, in its own way, an authoritative ministry of the word. Thanks to the unfailing succession of these three types of leadership, the Church can confidently bear witness to its Lord in every age and every culture.

All the ministries of the Church, as Paul repeatedly insists, are intended to build up the body of Christ and to equip it for its mission (1 Cor. 12:7; 14:5, 12, 26). They are means, not ends in themselves. The means whereby the Church is kept in the 'apostolic succession' include, in addition, activities such as the study of Scripture, prayer, and sacramental worship. In these pages we shall, however, consider only the three primary ministries, adverting to the distinctiveness of each, their mutual interplay, and their relationship to the original ministries. Since the three authoritative word-ministries belong to the common heritage of Christianity, we shall consider how they may help to overcome the existing divisions among separated Christian groups.

1. THE DISTINCTION OF MINISTRIES

(a) The Apostolic Ministry

The term 'apostle' in the New Testament has a variety of meanings. In the authentic

Pauline letters the apostles are missionaries sent out by the risen Jesus to proclaim the gospel, even at the price of suffering and persecution.[1] In many New Testament writings *the Twelve* are called apostles, presumably because they are shown as being commissioned to go forth and make disciples of all the nations (see Matt. 28:20), even though there is no historical evidence that all or even the majority of them did so. According to another New Testament view, found primarily in the early chapters of Acts, the Twelve 'apostles' were in general charge of the affairs of the Church.

When modern writers speak of the apostolicity of the Church they are usually referring either to its universal missionary thrust or to its perseverance in the apostolic faith. In discussions of ministry, however, apostolicity generally means the inheritance of the function of supreme oversight (*episkopē*) over the universal Church. By calling its highest office-holders successors of the apostles the Church reminds itself that in every age it needs to have trained, tested, and commissioned disciples who enter, in some sort, into the leadership functions of the Twelve. The Twelve, as described in the New Testament, exemplify the kind of self-effacing, vicarious authority that the Church attributes to its supreme pastors. Apostles speak in the name of him who sent them (see Luke 10:16, etc.).

The apostolic ministry of supervision is permanently necessary for the Church so that it may articulate its faith and co-ordinate its efforts as Christian mission may require. Without a unified authoritative leadership, the Church would disintegrate into a plurality of movements having, indeed, a certain common inspiration but incapable of adopting a clear corporate stand on any controversial issue.

(b) The Prophetic Ministry

In contrast to the other two kinds of leader here considered, the prophets in the Church owe their authority neither to their pastoral office nor to their academic skills, but rather to the free outpouring of the Spirit. The prophetic ministry is the work of the inspired imagination. Prophets teach neither by juridically binding decisions nor by probative arguments, but rather by proclamation and example. Enlightened from on high, the prophet moves out ahead of the community, bidding it follow along new or different lines. Not surprisingly, prophets are often rejected by their contemporaries. Suspected of undermining the institution, the prophet often falls into conflict with the official leadership. Yet in time the true prophet wins recognition and thus the entire Church becomes enriched with a new thematisation of the Christian message.

The prophetic charism defies institutionalisation. Although the Church has traditionally recognised charisms of office, there is no office in the Church that brings with it the gift of prophecy. It is quite possible for a prophet to be a bishop or even a pope, such as John XXIII in the opinion of many. But prophetic figures in our own century also include monks (Thomas Merton), secular priests (Max Metzger), and lay persons (Dorothy Day).

In Scripture and the history of religions we read of *prophetic orders and schools*. These institutions have rarely proved successful in the long run. The most that can be expected from them is to provide a discipline and an environment conducive to prophetic sensitivity. Thomas Merton believed that prophetic witness was integral to the monastic vocation in contemplative orders such as his own. Called out of the world to an existence radically different from that of humanity at large, the monk, he believed, was well positioned to see from God's point of view the fallacies of conventional human wisdom. Yet Merton acknowledged that the monasticism familiar to him did not measure up to its true vocation.[2]

If its task were simply to repeat verbatim a message given by Jesus himself, the Church might not need a succession of prophets. But it is commissioned to bear witness to Christ in a world very unlike that of biblical times. Prophets are needed to enable the Church to *discern the signs of the times*. As Schillebeeckx has shown, the prophetic experience is often fostered by close contact with men and women who are involved in humanly hopeless situations.[3] Many of the recent social documents of the Church come directly or indirectly out of an experienced familiarity with systemic evil.

(c) The Theological Ministry

Theologians and scholars in the Church have the responsibility to *reflect synthetically and critically on the Christian message*, bringing out its meaning and coherence. This ministry satisfies the human need to understand. In addition, it helps to correct aberrations and superstitions in the preaching and practice of the Church. This it does not by prophetic proclamation but by reasoned argument.

The First Vatican Council declared that when human reason, enlightened by faith, 'inquires earnestly, devoutly, and circumspectly, it attains, by God's gift, some understanding of mysteries, and that a most fruitful one'.[4] The Second Vatican Council spoke appreciatively of how scholars help to mature the judgment of the Church itself,[5] and in its Message to Men of Thought and Science exhorted scholars to have confidence in faith, 'this great friend of intelligence'.[6] Yet the critical observations of theology are often no more enthusiastically welcomed than the denunciations of the prophet. Theologians, too, are at times suspected of disloyalty to the institution.

Like the charism of prophecy, the charism of theology *can never be adequately institutionalised*. Some of the greatest theologians have been private scholars without a theological degree and without any canonical mission. The theologian, whose Christian faith and solidarity with the community of believers are normally presupposed, is formally constituted as a theologian by professional competence. Theologians are identified principally through recognition by their peers on the basis of scholarly achievement. Yet it may happen that a given theologian, ahead of his time, is not appreciated except by later generations.

2. CONVERGENCE AND TENSION

(a) A Concurrent Effort

Although not everything in the Church depends on the pastors, prophets, and theologians, their joint efforts over the centuries have done much to shape what we experience as Christianity:

> in the middle ages prophetic figures such as St Francis and St Dominic initiated movements that permeated the entire body of the Church, thanks in part to the great Franciscan and Dominican theologians who brought scholastic theology to its summit in the thirteenth century;
> in the sixteenth century the ecclesiological piety of prophetic reformers such as Ignatius of Loyola had a comparable influence on the scholastic revival and on the Catholicism of the Tridentine era;
> in our own century the prophetic ecumenism of John R. Mott, Charles H. Brent, and Paul Couturier prepared the paths for the World Council of Churches and Vatican Council II. The ecumenical theology of a Georges Florovsky, an Edmund Schlink, or an Yves Congar could scarcely have arisen except for the spiritual climate established by the ecumenical prophets who preceded them. Then, at the stage of implementation, ecumenical statesmen such as William A. Visser 't Hooft

and Augustin Cardinal Bea fashioned solid practical results on the basis of the pioneering work of their prophetic and theological predecessors.

As illustrated in these three historical examples, the life of Christians in the Church is moulded, in great part, by the concurrent efforts of prophets, scholars, and churchmen.

(*b*) Interdependence and Autonomy

For the progress of the Church it is crucial that the three classes of authoritative ministry here considered be open and receptive to one another. Paul himself pointed out the *mutual interdependence of the ministries* (1 Cor. 12:21-22). Each of the three vocations—the apostolic, the prophetic, and the theological—contains inbuilt hazards;

the apostolic leadership, left to itself, tends to encourage passive conformity and blind conservatism. Prelates are tempted to suppress troublesome questions. They tend to avoid new and provocative issues such as, in our day, the changing patterns of family life and sexual mores. Not everything new is worthy of approval, but new developments in secular society usually call for fresh responses on the part of the Church. A withdrawal from current experience could be detrimental to the overall apostolate;

the prophetic leaders can play an important corrective rôle with regard to the pastoral *magisterium*. But the prophets, caught up in their own insights, can easily become impatient and headstrong. They can fall into illusions, mistaking their own fantasies for the directives of the Holy Spirit. They therefore need to be assisted by the criticism of scholars and the discernment of pastors;

the intellectuals of the Church make an invaluable contribution to the preservation and development of Christian doctrine. Where would the Eastern Church be without Athanasius and the great Cappadocians, or the Western without Jerome and Augustine, and their successors? But the thinkers, with their love of speculation, are often inclined to neglect the spontaneous piety of the people and the practical wisdom of the pastoral leaders. They readily become infatuated with their own systems and neglectful of beliefs and practices that do not fit harmoniously into their own mental categories.

For *successful interaction, it is important that none of the three functions usurp the specialisation of the others or seek to reduce the others to innocuous servitude.* For theology or prophecy to perform its distinctive tasks it must retain a certain measure of autonomy and critical distance from the official leadership, while at the same time accepting the latter's supervision. There is wisdom in the medieval axiom, 'non ancilla nisi libera'. Scholars who criticise and prophets who denounce must not be hastily branded as heretics and apostates. The prelates must sometimes be prepared to accept correction as King David accepted the rebukes of Shimei: 'Let him alone, and let him curse, for the Lord has bidden him' (2 Sam. 16:11).

3. THE SUCCESSION

(*a*) *Successio Apostolorum*

The idea of succession is verified most strictly where there is a continuous, unbroken replacement of previous incumbents by others who follow them in the same office. For this reason it is not surprising that succession is discussed principally with reference to the official pastoral leadership, which is more highly institutionalised than the prophetic and scholarly functions. But even in the case of the pastoral office, talk of 'succession' is not unproblematic.

In the first place, there is a sense in which the apostles, as founders, have no successors. Others build on the foundations they have laid. The term *successio apostolorum* seems to imply that apostles succeed to apostles, but this is not in fact claimed. In episcopally ordered churches bishops are regarded as successors to the apostles, but even this opinion needs to be nuanced in view of the historical evidence. The bishops of the New Testament are local pastors without apparent responsibility for the oversight of the Church as a whole. The episcopal office—and especially the monarchical episcopate—did not become universal until the second or third century. *Nor does the New Testament provide direct evidence that any of the Twelve ever ordained bishops or looked on bishops as successors to the Twelve.* Thus the popular impression that the Twelve ordained bishops to take their place is, at best, an oversimplification. The view that bishops in the Catholic Church have orders stemming without interruption from the Twelve probably cannot be disproved but it seems highly improbable in the light of available historical evidence.

In recent theological literature the apostolic succession of pastoral leaders is often presented in a different light.[7] It is argued that the Church, in its fundamental reality as sacramentally representing Christ, has a plenitude of apostolic authority that is prior to, and hence independent of, its own canonical regulations. By virtue of this 'pre-canonical' power *the Church can structure its own pastoral office in certain specific ways.* It is not absolutely essential that the Church call its highest office-holders by the title of bishop or that they can be inducted into office by having other bishops impose hands on them. These canonical regulations, which currently have the force of law within the Roman Catholic Church, are not necessarily binding on all churches for all time.

The question as to the conditions under which the Catholic or Orthodox churches can partially or fully recognise the pastoral ministries in churches that lack the 'historic episcopate' is far too complicated to be treated in this essay. Much of the current literature maintains that the Church is not faced with a simple alternative between validity and invalidity.[8] Any church or ecclesial community, to the extent that it participates in the reality of the Church of Christ, has a capacity to confer spiritual power on its own pastors, even though these pastors be not ordained by bishops. This is not to claim, however, that all church polities are equally good or that all genuine Christian ministers have the same measure of ministerial power. According to a growing body of ecumenical opinion, the episcopal form of polity is to be esteemed as an efficacious sign of continuity and solidarity in the apostolic ministry.

(b) Successio Prophetarum

Because prophecy is not ordinarily transmitted by continuous succession or by induction into office, prophets do not 'succeed' their predecessors in an unbroken line as pastors commonly do.[9] Yet when the prophetic charism is bestowed, the recipient can become not simply a successor of the prophets but a prophet in the succession. Thus a *successio prophetarum* exists, even though it be *discontinuous and unpredictable.*

The unpredictable character of prophecy makes it possible for prophets to appear in alien environments, outside the limits of the old Israel or the Church. As Israel acknowledged the oracles of Balaam (Numbers, ch. 22-24), so the Church may be admonished through what Schillebeeckx calls 'foreign prophecy' (*Fremdprophetie*).[10] Although prophets often arouse conflict within their own communities, their voices are frequently recognised by outsiders. Roman Catholics, for instance, can acknowledge the prophetic endowments of a Soloviev or a Bonhoeffer, a Berdyaev or a Martin

Luther King. Protestants can be moved by the words or example of a John XXIII or a Teresa of Calcutta. Liberation theologians of different denominations find it easy to work in collaboration. Christians of all traditions, moreover, find it possible to draw inspiration from the deeds and doctrine of Mahatma Gandhi. In situations of institutional stagnation, the *successio prophetarum* can be a powerful force for promoting Christian unity and opening up communication with other living faiths.

(c) Successio Doctorum

Referring to the Pauline triad of ministries, modern authors often speak of the theologians as successors of the New Testament 'teachers'. But in fact we know little about these *didaskaloi*.[11] Were they experts in the Hebrew Scriptures, catechists, bearers of the Christian oral tradition, charismatic teachers, or missionary preachers? Whatever may have been the case, they do *not closely resemble the doctores of patristic times*. If one were to look for New Testament predecessors of Athanasius and Augustine, for instance, one might better turn to Paul and John than to the obscure, anonymous *didaskaloi*.

There is no automatic succession of theological masters in every generation. In times of cultural decline the Church may be, for some generations, without such leadership. At certain high moments of Christian learning, a whole constellation of *doctores* may appear at a given place and time, as happened, for instance, in Asia Minor at the end of the fourth century and in Paris in the thirteenth. In the early nineteenth century, when the sacred disciplines were at a relatively low ebb, the theological charism reappeared, thanks to a felicitous combination of circumstances, in many nations of Western Europe.

The theological charism, then, is neither bestowed by any official mandate or 'canonical mission', nor is it demolished by the removal of such a commission. It would be counterproductive for the Church to attempt to control theology by such institutional mechanisms, thus impairing the *relative autonomy of the theological enterprise*. The pastoral leadership, to be sure, has an obligation to warn against what it regards as errors and to resist heretical teaching.

Since the theological enterprise transcends all denominational frontiers, the *successio doctorum* is a reality of *ecumenical significance*. Few Catholics today question the theological competence of masters such as Luther, Calvin, Schleiermacher, and Barth. Nor do Protestants ignore the work of Augustine, Aquinas, Newman, and Rahner. In an age of organisational estrangement, the broader collegiality of theologians can help to establish intellectual communion among Christians of different traditions.

CONCLUSION

Ecclesial ruptures are usually occasioned by the lack of dialogue and mutual correction among the three ministries here considered. In most cases the blame must be shared among impatient reformers, doctrinaire theologians, and defensive prelates. For the prevention of schism and the restoration of unity it is important that pastors, prophets, and theologians be allowed to function with a measure of autonomy and that they be open to correction from one another. Any effort by one ministry to absorb or dominate the others can only aggravate the existing alienations.

It is a healthy sign that in recent decades the prophetic and theological enterprises have become highly ecumenical. Confessional differences, of course, continue to play a part, but they do not prevent communication across denominational lines. Mutual recognition among the pastoral leaders of different communities continues to be difficult to achieve, but further *progress may be expected if a free and open exchange is permitted among the three types of leader discussed in these pages, and if all alike are attentive to the movement of the Spirit in the Church as a whole.*

Notes

1. See R. E. Brown *Priest and Bishop: Biblical Reflections* (New York 1970) pp. 27, 59; also his 'Episkopē and Episkopos' *Theol. Studies* 41 (1980) 328.

2. On Merton as prophet see *Thomas Merton: Prophet in the Belly of a Paradox* ed. G. Twomey (New York 1978).

3. E. Schillebeeckx 'The Magisterium and the World of Politics' *Concilium* 36 (New York 1968) 19-39, esp. 29-31 (VI, 4 London 12-21).

4. Constitutio dogmatica *Dei Filius* cap. 4; DS 3016.

5. *Dei Verbum* § 12.

6. Sacrosanctum Oecumenicum Concilium Vaticanum II, *Constitutiones, Decreta, Declarationes* (Vatican City 1966) p. 1090. English translation *Documents of Vatican II* ed. W. A. Abbott (New York 1966) p. 731.

7. See, for example, K. Rahner *Vorfragen zu einem ökumenischen Amtsverständnis.* (Quaestiones Disputatae 65) (Freiburg 1974).

8. For a nuanced presentation of the various options see C. Vagaggini 'Possibilità e Limiti del riconoscimento dei ministeri non cattolici' in *Ministères et célébration de l'eucharistie* (Studia Anselmiana Fasc. 61) (Rome 1973).

9. As I have elsewhere pointed out, some of the early apologists regarded the permanence of prophecy as a mark of the true Church, but they did not apparently hold that the prophetic charism is normally transmitted from one prophet to another in a direct line. See A. Dulles 'The Succession of Prophets in the Church' *Concilium* 34 (New York 1968) 52-62, esp. 54-55 (IV, 4 London, pp. 28-32).

10. Schillebeeckx, in the article cited in note 3, p. 29.

11. See A. Van Ruler 'Is There a "Succession of Teachers"?' *Concilium* 34 (New York 1968) 63-73 (IV, 4 London, pp. 33-37).

Yves Congar

VI. Towards a Catholic Synthesis

THERE WERE, to my mind, two ways of thinking about and writing this concluding article. I could on the one hand, treat the theme of this number by itself, and I should do so from the point of view of a Catholic theologian but in an ecumenical perspective. Alternatively, I could make a synthesis out of the preceding articles and here again in a Catholic and ecumenical manner. But within the time allowed me I received and was able to read only the articles written by L. Vischer, U. Kühn, O. Engstrøm, L. Sartori, G. Daly and L. Boff. I therefore decided to combine the two possible ways whilst in fact giving priority to the former.

The first thing that made me pause was the very title: 'Who has the say in the Church?' There are various forms of say, various modes of utterance. Liturgical celebration is one of them, but so is what we actually do in life. Any one of the faithful can found a movement, an institution, a religious society (subject to having it approved). He or she can practise theology and publish his or her thoughts. The directors of this issue seem rather to have had in mind the relationship between theologians and the 'magisterium', which can be in conflict. This is obviously a very important element in the question 'Who has the say in the Church?' But what do we mean by Church? Everybody has his own definition and six non-Roman Catholic authors were invited to make their own response. For me the Church is the Roman Catholic Church, but an ecumenical concern bids us allow others to have their say. In this sense they too have a say amongst us, without canonical status or official rights. Did not K. Barth and D. Bonhoeffer speak in the 'Church'?

1. NORMS

(a) Truth in Christ

What we are talking about is not just any say but a Christian say: St Paul would have talked about speaking 'in Christ'. It is a matter of saying something that helps the Church live in the truth. We have moved beyond the classical and purely philosophical notion of truth and we have since Vatican II rediscovered the originality of the theologal, at once biblical and theological, notion of truth. The truth we are now talking about is *saving truth*, the truth God manifested by deeds (the events of the history of salvation) and words. It comes to its fullest expression *in Christ*, Word made flesh. It is witnessed to in the preaching of the prophets and apostles, in what they did, and in the writings which God led them to leave us 'nostrae salutis causae',[1] for the sake of our salvation. The Holy Spirit leads us into all truth (John 16:13) by making us confess the mystery of Christ the Lord (1 Cor. 12:3). The category that must govern all our research is that of 'life in the truth of Christ', not that of infallibility. Infallibility—a terribly weighted term which we need to use very warily—is a function of truth. We must not make infallibility the foundation stone of our structures and make truth a function of it.

(b) Regula Fidei

God alone is absolute truth. God alone is infallible of himself. He communicates his truth through *his Word and his Breath.* The two act jointly. 'The Scriptures are perfect because they have been uttered by the Word of God and by his Spirit' (St Irenaeus *Adversus Haereses* IV, 2, 3). What God communicates to us is for the Church a source of life in the truth. It is preserved in the truth by the fidelity with which it adheres to this communication, that is to say, to the objective rule which comes to it from the apostles. For St Irenaeus this rule 'has many names which all have the same content: rule of truth, rule of faith (*kanōn* or *hypothesis*), body of truth, true knowledge, preaching of the truth, faith, tradition of the apostles, the doctrine of the apostles, the charism of truth. We should note that the term "rule" refers not to some external measure, a criterion that enables us to establish the truth, but truth itself. In the same way preaching designates the object preached, tradition, what is actually handed on, and even the "charism of truth" is not a gift of perceiving the truth (something like the gift of infallibility) but truth itself.'[2] If there is some regulating authority in the Church, that authority is itself subject to regulation. What is primary is the *traditum*, what is handed on, and it governs the *actus tradendi*, the actual handing on. As St Irenaeus puts it so magnificently and memorably in *Adversus Haereses* III, 24, 1, it is the precious deposit which renews the vase which contains it. St Athanasius calls the Symbol of Nicaea 'the faith professed by the Fathers in accordance with the Scriptures' (*Ad Epictetum* 1, P.G. 26,104). We cannot exaggerate the importance of this point for our purposes here. We are too inclined to think of things in bipolar terms: in terms of the faithful (the theologians) and hierarchic authority. But both these terms are governed, regulated and given life by the *traditum* in which the canonical Scriptures are the *norma normans, non normata* 'for, inspired by God and committed once and for all to writing, they impart the Word of God himself without change, and make the voice of the Holy Spirit resound in the words of the prophets and apostles'.[3]

(c) Tradition and reactualisation

The unique *traditum* given to the saints once and for all (Jude 3) is handed on by an *actus tradendi* which takes on the dimensions of time and space, and which is, therefore, visible, historical and co-extensive with the life of the Church. It is the very life of the Church.[4] The Church must be making saving truth present time and time again in response to needs and demands and so be interpreting it in such a way that the unique and identical saving truth finds diverse expression. This is the way in which a treasury of such expressions comes into being in the shape of liturgies, councils, the writings of the Fathers, the decisions of pastoral authorities, the works of theologians, the life of the faithful. . . . St Athanasius speaks again in the Church every time it confesses the divinity of the Holy Spirit, St Basil and the Council of 381 every time it confesses the divinity of Christ, St Augustine every time it affirms the gracious initiative of God in our faith. Luther continues to speak in the church of the confession of Augsburg, Calvin in the church of the Reform. This is how we can say, in the terms of the Faith and Order conference in Montreal (1965), that each church receives the Tradition (with a big T: the *Traditum*) in and through the traditions (with a little t: the history specific to each). At the same time the dogmas and the first developments—the four or six first councils, the first five centuries—are common to all. The way of referring to them is, however, not exactly the same. The Protestant churches profess constantly to submit their preaching, their theologians, their reformers and their confessions of faith themselves to the judgment of the Word of God, that is to say, the Scriptures. This leads them to start afresh all the time and successively to follow different currents. The Catholic Church also maintains the criterion of the Scriptures but it believes in a homogeneous development of its life and of the word of its teaching authority. As for the Eastern Church, which is often called the church of the Fathers or of the seven councils, it lives in a sort of immediacy to the past authorities which are always present to it.

(d) Historicity

We need to note *the historicity of every human conception and word*. This applies even to the dogmas of the councils, the very texts of the Scriptures. This does not relativise truth itself: what is true is definitively true. It relativises only our approach to the truth. We do in fact approach truth, we do not attain it in one go, we gain it. We need time, a series of attempts, exchange with others and their contributions. G. *Daly's* observations become relevant here. Even conciliar definitions are perfectible. We cannot speak against them but we can go beyond them. Ignorance of history turns dogma into 'dogmatism' and ideology, which are its besetting vices.[5] Thus interchange and groping are inevitable but these also involve tension. The process of welding all this into something beneficial takes time. Wanting to come to a conclusion too soon risks failing to absorb complementary values. Truth is symphonic (Hans Urs von Balthasar).

2. 'TEACHING CHURCH', 'CHURCH TAUGHT'?

(a) Differentiation

The whole people of God preserves the *Tradition*, celebrates and lives the truth received from the apostles. The whole Church is apostolic. The whole body is given life by the Spirit which distributes its charisms throughout it, that is to say, talents and gifts of grace (see Rom. 12:6). But the body has a structure, it is organised. Christ established apostles, prophets, evangelists in it, and the Letter to the Ephesians adds that pastors and teachers are 'for the equipment of the saints, for the work of the ministry, for building up the body of Christ' (4:12). From the time of the apostles the community, alive as a whole, has been internally differentiated: if there are pastors, there is flock[6] or 'the brethren'.[7] This differentiation within the 'brotherhood' in due course developed into:

(i) a distinction between clergy and laity, a distinction which was clear from the third century onwards but which came to take on the proportions of a fundamental juridical structure for those who disregarded it: 'Ordo ex Christi institutione clericos a laicis in Ecclesia distinguit' ('By Christ's institution order distinguishes the clergy from the laity in the Church');[8]

(ii) the massive and oft-repeated affirmation, especially from the time of Gregory XVI onwards, of the fact that the Church is a 'societas inaequalis, hierarchica'.[9] From then on, until Vatican II, this assertion became fundamental;

(iii) the distinction, expressed in various analogical ways, between 'teaching Church' and 'Church taught'. Apart from certain anticipations on the part of anti-Protestant controversialists, the initial context of this distinction seems to have been the reaction to Jansenist ecclesiology and to the refusal of the bull *Unigenitus*. It was current towards 1750 and in the catechisms at the beginning of the nineteenth century.[10] It was generally tied to a distinction between the 'infallibilitas in docendo' ascribed to the body of bishops united with the pope and the 'infallibilitas in credendo' attributed to the faithful.[11] It is clear that this distinction needs to be carefully understood.

(b) Without opposition

The bias of these distinctions, their heavily juridical form and the importance they came to have derived from the necessity, in itself salutary, of allowing the Church an autonomous law and of ensuring its existence effectively against the claims of princes. This was the inspiration of the reform of the eleventh century (Leo IX and Gregory VII). This brought a reinforcement of the law of celibacy for priests in its wake. We should like to think that the fact that the East did not experience this struggle and that imperial power continued to take responsibility, 'symbolically', for large areas of the social life of the Church, has something to do with the particular genius the East has for uniting clergy and layfolk together in a vital way that is its particular pride. Not that I wish by these remarks to belittle the depth of the anthropological and ecclesiological doctrine of 'Sobornost'.

We go along with the criticisms *Leonardo Boff* makes of the distinction, at least when it becomes an opposition, between 'teaching Church' and 'Church taught'. His dialectical approach is very interesting. Should we, by way of a foil, cite some of the strictly monstrous but significant expressions of an attitude which used to be widely held? Here are two examples: 'The passive infallibility of the faithful thus consists in listening as one should to the *magisterium*.'[12] 'Are not the parish priest the Church taught in regard to the bishop and the bishop in regard to the pope, like the faithful?'[13]

It was ideas like this that drew Tyrell's fire against the Church that was infallible 'because she possesses an infallible Pope—much as a flock of sheep in union with its shepherd might be called intelligent'.[14] But let us leave caricatures aside. We can avoid them if we think of a single Church which as a whole listens, celebrates, loves, confesses, and in which each member is challenged to exercise his or her function. *It is the whole Church that learns, it is the whole Church that teaches, but in different ways.* The Fathers testify to this verity in abundance.[15] The secret of a balanced position is expressed in the formula which St Augustine often repeated in different guises: 'Vobis sum episcopus, vobiscum Christianus', 'I am a bishop for you, a Christian with you'.[16] Before H. Schell Dom Gréa showed that the model of this life of the Church lay in the Trinity.[17] The Persons exist for each other, with one another, within each other. Between them they as it were form a council, realise a 'concelebration', said Gréa.

It follows that in the Church each and everyone has the say. But under what conditions, in what way? This is what we must now go on to see, although we shall have to do so bit by bit, with the consequent risk that we shall in the very process of analysis and noting differences lose sight of the organic unity which we have just stressed.

3. THE CHURCH SPEAKS THROUGH ITS INSTITUTIONS, THROUGH ITS HISTORY

(a) *The liturgy is no doubt the most important way in which the Church speaks.* Here the Church lives at full stretch and in its purest form. Edmund Schlink once pointed out

F

that dogmatic formulations in the Bible are often found in the context of doxologies.[18] The Church celebrates its mysteries and expresses its faith through this celebration. St Thomas characterises worship as a 'protestatio fidei', a proclamation of faith. If I celebrate Easter I cannot doubt either the redemption or the resurrection. If I celebrate the annunciation, I cannot doubt the incarnation. St Cyril of Alexandria sent Nestorius the Nicene Creed and wrote: 'Here is the faith of the Catholic and Apostolic Church which the orthodox bishops of East and West unanimously confess in their praises'.[19] The Marian feasts in effect constitute that 'Christological auxiliary' of which K. Barth spoke. The feasts of the saints express the truth of the mystical Body and faith in everlasting life. They also give the Church an atmosphere of warmth that no merely theoretical word can achieve. The eucharistic anaphoras are great doxologies and anamneses. In 1978 the bishops of France were able to publish a great profession of faith by way of a commentary on the fourth eucharistic prayer. As for the sacraments, they are actions, but also word—not only because they include words but because they are celebrations. Just think what the celebration of the Eucharist *says*, what the rites of marriage and ordination *say*. . . . To take the example of the funeral of Paul VI, what an expressive gesture the arrangements and ceremonial were!

(b) *Institutions also speak.* Schools, hospitals, for example, or the property of the Church. The world sees all this and assesses the Church accordingly. The internal institutions and structures speak within the Church independently of what they may actually be saying, even as institutions or structures of a certain sort. Think of the episcopal function, of episcopal conferences, of synods. The bishop of Rome alone speaks more loudly than other bishops, and that by his mere existence and style, independently of what he may say. He has a symbolic function, he personifies Catholic unity and identity. Disposed round him, the curia, the secretariats, the central organisations also speak. Their style, their methods of work say something by themselves. What interested the public in the affairs of Küng and Schillbeeckx was the procedures rather than the doctrinal issues, even though the former were sometimes ill enough understood. Reactions to *Opus Dei* show the same thing. The ways in which human rights are exercised, religious use money, forgiveness and reconciliation are concretely practised, women are treated—and so on—are all examples of how the manner in which things are done and seen to be done is in practice more important than what is said about them. *Facts* may even clash with words. *They have their own eloquence.*

4. THE FAITHFUL SPEAK. 'SENSUS FIDEI', 'SENSUS FIDELIUM'

(a) **The lay commitment**

The way in which we dealt with this question in 1953 (see note 15) is now outdated. We did so under the sign or in the light of a division between what belongs to the clergy as teachers—the public domain—and the private domain. Today we are all concerned with the construction of the Church, with testifying to the gospel. The faithful do more than just express themselves in informal groups: they there find it possible to speak freely and so make their Christian word or the expression of their prayer coincide with what they really are and do. Apart from the very radical groups, such groups want to be Christian and do not deny that they belong to the Church. Many of the faithful are active in domains which are formally, and even officially the Church: catechesis, including a share in the creation of the forms thereof, the animation of parishes and Sunday assemblies without a priest, pastoral councils. . . .

The fact that many of the faithful study theology, although still rarely teach and particularly produce it, is new and promising. In France two theological journals of high quality are directed and largely edited by layfolk: *Les Quatres Fleuves* and *Communio*. At the bottom of all this is the sentiment of being the People of God which is concerned to serve the cause of the gospel as one whole: 'nostra res agitur', 'we're in this together'. It is no longer just the business of the clergy with their little circle. We are all called to serve, though clearly in different ways. In this connection people sometimes talk of the democratisation of the Church (see *Concilium* 63 (1971); in France this term has too political a flavour to be much used). It would be better to speak of brotherhood. At the same time it cannot be denied that the general climate does have an impact on the way we live in the Church. Human beings today want to take personal responsibility for what they profess. They want their say and they want to be heard wherever they want to take an active part in the decision that concern them. Underlying all this is a new sense of truth, akin to the feeling for authenticity: we commit ourselves where we feel we are recognised; truth is what enables us to place ourselves in the world in relation to others and to ourselves.

(b) Public opinion in the Church

This is what explains so many manifestations of opinion or protest. Public opinion, at least that of defined groups, is expressing itself in a new fashion in the Church and in church matters. There are numerous studies or articles in this subject or on 'free speech in the Church', to which reference may be made. Opinion has long been a factor. It has been observed that certain decisions of the popes over the temporal authority of kings—for example, the power to depose them—vanished as soon as they lost popular support. Daily opinion conditions the exercise of the most authoritarian powers and can prevent the application of certain laws.[20] Public opinion really came into its own during the nineteenth century. In regard to Church matters, pastors reacted, as Monsignor Dupanloup did, for example, against Louis Veuillot. But Emile Ollivier, head of the liberal government, came back at him:

> The pamphleteering prelate loses no opportunity to rebuke journalists and complains that, layfolk as they are, they do not leave delicate questions, most intimate, serious and inside questions to the bishops. This is a surprising reproach. Are lay people not members of the Church? Can they remain indifferent to the conflicts of the spiritual society in which they live? If it is interest that creates competence, has one any right to exclude them from any questions except those they have not taken the trouble to study? They have as a matter of dogma been excluded from any share in the government of the Church and in the definition of dogmas, as a matter of diplomacy had their privilege in the election of bishops transferred to princes; but they have created religious journalism and they have in this way, in our age of publicity and discussion, established for themselves a power of their own which is greater than any they have had refused or withdrawn. Abuses apart, what is regrettable about this development?[21]

Abuses or sharp practices are, of course, possible, indeed real enough: pressure groups, indiscretions invading personal integrity, the tendency to emphasise the superficial or the sensational, if not the downright scandalous. We understand, because we are involved ourselves, when a churchman suffers from the power of this base currency. All the media are implicated today. The solution does not consist in the imposition of a censorship that limits freedom of speech or the expression of opinion. Our highest authorities have acknowledged their legitimacy and even their necessity.[22] The problem is in the first place one of *information* and therefore also of *communication*. People have talked of a right to information. Distortions of opinion and of its expression may well reflect distortions at the level of information.

(c) What Christians do

L. Sartori has dealt with the 'sensus fidelium'. This is also a subject on which a great deal has been written.[23] This term covers two things that are related but do not coincide. On the one hand, there is the *sensus fidei*, which is a quality inherent in a *subject*, on whom the grace of faith, charity, the gifts of the Spirit confer *a faculty of perceiving the truth of the faith and of discerning anything opposed to it*. The *sensus fidelium*, on the other hand, is what can be grasped from outside, objectively, about *what the faithful, and especially layfolk, believe and profess*. It tends towards a consensus, which can only be partial. Such a consensus, when it expresses itself, is akin to public opinion. It is clear that where Christianity is concerned the sense of the faith cannot be individualist; it is conditioned by the authenticity of a life in community. A Christian is not a Christian alone; he is assured of holding the truth only in the Church.

Möhler and Newman loved to cite Hippolytus' 'phronēma ecclesiastikon', Vincent of Lerins' 'ecclesiae intelligentiae auctoritas'. We consider that the Holy Spirit—the 'Holy One', says *Lumen Gentium* § 12, with reference to 1 John 2:20-27—ensures the *sensus fidei* of the people of God in so far as it is possessed of a universal consensus along with its pastors and is indefectibly attached to the apostolic faith. We must not idealise the *sensus fidei* of individuals or particular groups too much: the socio-psychological tests used by J. P. Deconchy disclose the influence of psychological and social conditioning.[24] Fervent but directionless communities can deviate or slip into syncretism. . . .

We do, however, attach great value to what Christians *declare by their behaviour* when they risk their peace, or the pleasures or amenities of life, even life itself, in order to testify to the gospel and seek to realise society's needs, especially in situations of oppression and injustice. This is what gives 'theologies of liberation' their original epistemological status: the practice of a Christian and poor people fertilises thought. See *Concilium* 96 (1974). The blood of witnesses guarantees the seriousness involved. The Church of our time has once again become a Church of martyrs. This supreme witness is also a word. 'Who speaks in the Church?' Witnesses, martyrs. And the second line is constituted by those who speak for the cause for example, Justice and Peace Commissions at the Roman or national level. They have often spoken a Christian word in the Church and in the world.

5. THEOLOGIANS[25]

Theologians are members of the body of the faithful who, as such, are caught up in the confession of the apostolic faith and whose business it is to speak. And about what? About God, *theo-logein*, but in a specific manner which distinguishes them alike from the simple faithful with their naive faith and from the members of the pastoral hierarchy and ordinary preachers. The New Testament knows a ministry (*diakonia*) of the word which includes all the forms of its exercise.[26] It also knows, as the primitive Church does, a specific service of teachers, *didaskaloi*.[27] Theologians continue this service. Their particular way of doing this is to use the resources of human reason in order to articulate questions and responses issuing from the human spirit: philological, historical, critical resources. . . . *The theologians' domain is, therefore, that of interpretation*, which is practised at different levels.

(a) The given

The first such level is that of the given, the datum: *Scripture, witnesses of the Tradition, formulations of the magisterium*. These documents have been composed in a certain language issuing from a particular cultural setting and historical and social context. The theologian goes beyond a naive reading and offers a maturely critical understanding and a re-rendering that meets the needs of the educated world today. We should no doubt say: the educated worlds today, in the plural, seeing that we have left behind the relative homogeneity of the classical eras, quite apart from the fact that East has always been distinct from the West.

The given comes in bulk, not sorted and packed. This is true of the Scriptures but also of the documents of Tradition—a broad river silted with the charge of ages!—and even some utterances of the *magisterium* which do not always agree among themselves. Interpretation seeks to make them coherent and to construct an ordered discourse out of them. This will involve a choice. There is a whole range of 'biblical theologies', christologies, etc. The message elaborated in this way then has to be translated into the language and terms of our resources today. To the extent that a theologian is not content merely to please himself but to perform a service for the Church he is called upon to *present the message in such a way that it makes sense for his contemporaries*. This is why 'fundamental theology' has become so important in our time.

(b) Freedom of research

This job of interpretation, including the interpretation of the pronouncements of the *magisterium*, is near enough what Newman attributed to the 'school of theologians', *schola theologorum*, as he called it. It was concerned to explain or interpret these pronouncements and, in general, those of the Tradition, to make their meaning and scope but also their limits clearer. It is in this sense that Newman saw in the 'schola theologorum' the 'regulating principle of the Church'.[28] This was saying a lot. At the same time this task has become more complicated since Newman. History was already speaking in his time, and the tools of evaluation at our disposal are even more refined (the sociology of knowledge, for example), and we include questions put and contributions made by non-Roman communions, the Orthodox, the Reformed. We take them seriously. It follows that truth no longer depends only on an obedience to what is established, it ventures forward into uncharted and undefined country.

We do not endorse risky ventures and still less any that deviate from the firm affirmations of the confessors of the apostolic faith, but we understand only too well that there will inevitably, even normally, be tensions between certain theologians and pastoral authorities, or between such theologians and members of the faithful accustomed to received ways of speech which they take for the Tradition. The issue here is that of freedom of research and its expression for theologians. Everybody proclaims this freedom, often with the rider that this freedom must be 'just' or 'legitimate', which suggests a limit and conditions. 'The theologian is a free and responsible person, but free with the freedom of the Christian, which expresses itself in an openness to the light granted by the faith and guaranteed by fidelity to the Church.'[29] The principle is unarguable. The application may well not be easy when one works in what the *Concilium declaration* of 29 November 1979 called the 'advance posts of the faith where it is difficult to sustain the service of the understanding of the faith today especially so far as relations with the human sciences are concerned, and where it must be possible to do research for a long time, to make mistakes, and to learn from one's mistakes in the light of other people's criticism and work'. Research, by very definition, implies that the theologian *cannot be content to respect and comment on what has been achieved and rounded out, to gloss and justify official language.* Besides which the latter has often enough made use of one theology amongst others which as such has not the same authority as a direct expression of faith.

6. PASTORAL AUTHORITY

It is not just that pastoral authority has a say, but rather that *speaking in the form of preaching the word is its first duty*.[30] Whereas the characteristic of theological work is the fact that it questions, it is the business of the pastoral authorities, of the body of bishops, to affirm, testify to and perpetuate the testimony of the apostles. This cannot be done without some elaboration or reasoning, as we see in the case of the very apostles themselves, but the bishop's essential rôle is to maintain and propagate the apostolic testimony through which the faith, and therefore the Church, is built up. The Church is planted not by the theologians but by the bishops.

(a) Authentic *magisterium*

According to certain modern presentations before the Council it seemed that the ideal way of exercising pastoral authority, which for all practical purposes meant the pope, was that of 'defining', decreeing. But definition, especially when what is in question is the mystery of God, is a formidable act to which we should resort only when compelled to do so in order to safeguard the truth of religion and the confession of faith. Vatican I had proclaimed the irreformability or the infallibility of the papal *magisterium* in its solemn and extraordinary exercise. It had not determined—could it have done so?—the quality of its ordinary teaching. What happened in practice was that people who were more docile than enlightened then *in practice ascribed the quality of the pope's extraordinary teaching to his ordinary teaching*. Although it made this distinction, the encyclical *Humani generis* of 1950 could seem to exacerbate this confusion.[31] One cannot treat the 'he who hears you hears me' of Luke 10:16 as the foundation for a juridical structure and as the grant of absolute value to authority, whatever it does and says. The value involved is conditioned by the object and the content. The very texts of the *magisterium* itself never cease asserting that the *magisterium* is helped to guard and teach *pure et integre* only 'id quod traditum est', 'what has been handed down'.[32] We know the words of *Dei Verbum* § 10: 'Quod quidem Magisterium non supra verbum Dei est . . . pie audit, sancte custodit et fideliter exponit . . .', 'The *magisterium* is not above the Word of God . . . it listens to it devoutly, guards it religiously, and explains it faithfully'. The criterion of truth is that 'id quod traditum est'; the *magisterium* of the Church is fundamentally a *magisterium* of Truth itself.

Nevertheless, in the sacramental structure of the Church, 'office itself has something charismatic about it. It includes something that goes beyond it'.[33] That is why it embodies in itself and as an authority in the society of the Church a value of its own. This is what is expressed in the term 'authentic teachers', which *Lumen Gentium* § 25 explains as follows: 'endowed with the authority of Christ, who preach to the people committed to them the faith they must believe and put into practice'. *Die verbum* § 10 says in a similar vein: 'The task of authentically interpreting the word of God, whether written or handed on, has been entrusted exclusively to the living teaching office of the Church, whose authority is exercised in the name of Jesus Christ'. The word authority is here taken in a juridical sense, not in the subjective and moral sense highlighted by Gabriel Daly. We do not, unfortunately, to our knowledge have a monograph on the precise sense and uses of this term in ecclesiology. In juridical usage it means 'original', 'originally'. In ecclesiastical and medieval Latin it designates the quality attached to the author, what is endowed with authority. Here it means: Which embodies an authority derived from that which Christ imparted to the teaching mission given to the apostles. It has a value proper to supernatural authority but, of course, tied to the saving truth communicated by God, justified and regulated by the service of this truth. *Now it is clear that the recognition of this truth is not a monopoly of the body of bishops.* The latter cannot be isolated from the whole Church in which theologians work.

(b) Pastoral *magisterium*

Besides which there are many levels of exercise of the *magisterium*. Pius XII used the term (did he invent it?) 'pastoral magisterium'. It is the exercise of pastoral responsibility in concrete circumstances. It is inductive rather than deductive, tied to what we know; it is also prospective, open to what has to be done. Examples would be John XXIII's encyclical *Pacem in terris* and Paul VI's letter *Octogesima adveniens*. Below the level of doctrinal pronouncements, pastoral authority speaks by decisions belonging to its governing rôle.

Who has the say in the Church: first and most clearly of all, the bishops, and first and foremost amongst them the bishop of Rome, successor of Peter. In the gospels and Acts, Peter speaks repeatedly on behalf of the apostles. He has a representative quality, he embodies and personifies the group. There is an interesting phenomenon here, an instance of a very important relationship in ecclesiology, that between 'the one and the many'. By the same token, however, this means that the pope is never alone—and we know that the Prefatory Note of Explanation to the evaluation of the votes on Chapter III of *Lumen Gentium* deliberately said 'seorsim', 'by himself', and not 'solus', 'alone'. That is why the expression 'without the consent of the Church' used at Vatican I continues to be regrettable, despite the clearest explanation about the exact meaning given of it. For 'consensus Ecclesiae' had a positive meaning and use which the dogma of Vatican I did not affect. We do not here need to sum up the treatises about the theological criteria of the different forms of episcopal and pontifical utterances. There are many such treatises. As far as we know, none of them does justice to what we know through the historical sciences.

7. ECUMENICAL CONVERGENCES

Two major questions have been put in this issue: Who has the say, what is the attitude of the churches in this regard? and: How are they maintained in the truth?

As regards the first question, the document on Faith and Order represents a good description of the state of affairs in the different churches, but its precision comes out only if one is already well-informed and can supply names, facts and theologies in every paragraph. All Christian communions comprise the same components but in different proportions: *a people, theologians, ministers and the exercise of magisterium. Ulrich Kühn* is not the only person to speak of a qualified teaching ministry in the churches of the Reform, which does equal justice to personal conscience and the community setting.[34] There are even proceedings on the ground of doctrine in the Lutheran church.[35] It is well known that in the Orthodox Church primacy is given to truth itself, as discerned in the agreement of the whole Church and that a decisive weight is given to holiness.[36] On the other hand, in the Roman Catholic Church, where insistence on the *magisterium* has been so strong and has sometimes taken on juridical forms, the royal and priestly people does make itself heard; we know the importance of *reception*[37] and the *apostolicity of the content* is the internal norm of the apostolicity or formal legitimacy of ministry.[38]

All Christian communities are conscious of being maintained in the saving truth. Vatican II acknowledged that they are maintained by the *Holy Spirit* to the extent that they are so maintained: 'vera quaedam in Spiritu Sancto coniunctio . . . et quosdem illorum usque ad sanguinis effusionem roboravit',[39] 'in some real way they are joined with us in the Holy Spirit. . . . Some indeed he has strengthened to the extent of the shedding of their blood'. All Christians who have not lost it are animated by the same movement of openness and gift to God, through Christ, in the Holy Spirit, which is the 'fides qua creditur', the faith by which we believe. This faith does, of course have a content, faith in the sense of believing, the 'fides quae creditur', the faith which is believed, and this is not wholly the same from one communion to another. Nevertheless the *unity of the fides qua*, the faith by which we believe, *entails a certain unity of the fides quae*, the faith which is believed. Attempts have been made to delimit the latter in various ways: in terms of fundamental articles, a 'quinquecentennial consensus', the first four or six councils, the undivided Church, etc. None of these norms is satisfactory, and yet none of them is without value; they express a reality in which ecumenism lives. They are the concrete basis of the common testimony of which the Faith and Order report speaks.

Doctrinal Agreements have been signed, at least by official commissions of theologians, on many decisive topics, amongst them the most delicate. These can be illustrated by the Malta Report on Church and Gospel in 1971, and a text on the Eucharist in 1978 between the Roman Catholic Church and the World Lutheran Federation. As between the Anglican communion and the Roman Catholic Church there have been the agreed statements on the Eucharist in 1971, on ministries in 1973, and on authority in the Church in 1976. Then there was the agreed report on 'The Presence of Christ in the Church and in the World' in 1976 on the part of the Catholic Church and the World Reformed Alliance. Faith and Order put together a largely agreed statement on baptism, ministry and Eucharist. We know that theological dialogue has started between the Roman Catholic Church and the Orthodox after fifteen years of the dialogue of charity. And finally a common confession of christological faith has been promulgated by Rome and the non-Chalcedonian churches; this professes the Chalcedonian faith in terms other than those on which there was divergence (Paul VI with Shenouda III of Alexandria, on 10 May 1973, and also with Vasken III, of Armenia, and Yakoub III, of Syria). The Orthodox Church is following a similar path.

In this way being maintained in the truth tends towards a unity of confession of the truth. This is a unity which it is being more and more widely acknowledged will not be uniform either in its expression or even in the internal structure and emphases of the component parts. It seems to me that the major ecumenical question for us today is precisely this question as to how much diversity is compatible with communion. *Truth is symphonic*. The conductor is the Spirit of truth. Who better to speak in the Church and to bring us into or keep us in the truth?

Translated by John Maxwell

Notes

1. The originality of this saving truth is well brought out by, among others: W. Kayer *Dogme et evangile* (Paris 1967); I. de la Potterie 'La Vérité de la sainte Ecriture et l'Histoire du salut de'après la Const. dogm. "Dei Verbum"' *Nouv, Rev. Théol.* 98 (1966) 149-189; M.-D. Chenu 'Vérité évangelique et metaphysique wolfienne à Vatican II' *Rev. Sc. phil., théol.* 57 (1973) 632-640; J. J.

Alemany and M. A. Acebal 'Salus en la Const. Dei Verbum. Estudio comparativo de sus cinco redacciones' *Rev. Esp. de Teol.* 38 (1978) 141-167. See *Dei verbum* §§ 2, 7, 11.

2. B. Reynders in *L'Infaillibilité de l'Eglise.* Journées oecumeniques de Chevetogne, 25-29 septembre 1961 (Chevetogne 1963) pp. 34-35. And see D. van den Eynde *Les Normes de l'enseignement chrétien dans la littérature patristique des trois premiers siècles* (1933) p. 283.

3. Dogmatic Constitution *Dei verbum* VI § 21.

4. *Dei verbum* § 8 puts it very well: 'Sicque Ecclesia, in sua doctrina, vita et cultu, perpetuat cuntisque generationibus transmittit omne quod ipse est, omne quod credit'.

5. J. Nolte *Dogma in Geshichte. Versuch einer Kritik des Dogmatismus in der Glaubensdarstellung* (Freiburg 1971).

6. Acts 20:28; 1 Pet. 5:2 and 3.

7. Acts 11:1 (v. 2 in Codex D); 12:17; 15:1; 21:17-18.

8. Codex Iuris Canonici can. 948. The sources refer back to Innocent III—the profession of faith imposed on the Waldenses (letter of 18 December 1208 to the archbishop of Tarragona: Reg. XI, 196)—and to the Council of Trent, sess. XXIII, c. 4.

9. References may be found in our contribution to the colloquium *Ecclesiam Suam* (Rome 1980): 'Situation écclesiologique au moment de "Ecclesiam suam" et passage à une Eglise dans l'itinéraire des hommes'.

10. Ch. van der Plancke 'Une Conscience d'Eglise à travers la catéchèse janséniste du XVIIIe siècle' *Rev. Hist. écclés.* 72 (1977) 5-39; Y. Congar *L'Eglise de St Augustin: l'époque moderne* (Paris 1970), end of Ch. XII.

11. See G. Thils 'L'Infaillibilité de l'Eglise "in credendo" and "in docendo" ' *Salesianum* 24 (1962) 298-335; *L'Infaillibilité du peuple chrétien 'in credendo'. Notes de théologie post-tridentine* (Louvain 1963).

12. A. A. Goupil *La Règle de foi*, n. 17, 2nd ed. (Paris 1941) p. 48. Other references may be found in our *Jalons pour une thèologie du laicat* (Paris 1953) p. 400, n. 77.

13. *Le Rôle des laics dans l'Eglise. Carrefour 1952* (Montreal 1952) p. 9.

14. *Medievalism* (London 1908) p. 86.

15. We cited many of them in Ch. VI of *Jalons pour une théologie du laicat* 'Les Laics et la fonction prophétique de l'Eglise'. The edition of 1964 carries additions on pp. 650-659.

16. *Sermo 340*, 1 (PL 38, 1485) et very often. Or else 'condiscipulus'.

17. Schell *Katholische Dogmatik* III/I, pp. 382-385; A. Gréa *De l'Eglise et de sa divine constitution.* Book I, Ch. 8 § 4.

18. E. Schlink 'Die Struktur der dogmatischen Aussage als ökumenisches Problem' *Kerygma u. Dogma* 3 (1957) 251-306 (265 ff.).

19. *Acta Conc. Oec.* I, 1, 1 p. 34; PG 77, 109.

20. L. Leclerq *Leçons de droit naturel* I, no. 46; II no. 13. The example given is that of tsarist power in 1849.

21. E. Ollivier *L'Eglise et l'Etat au concile du Vatican* 2nd ed. (1879) p. 446.

22. Pius XII, address to the journalists, 17 February 1950 (AAS 42, 1950, 251, 256); John XXIII, address to the press, 6 June 1962; *Lumen Gentium* § 37; Cardinal Cigognani, letter of 2 July 1966, to the 53rd. Semaine sociale de France (Nice).

23. The references given by Sartori may be supplemented by the following: W. Beinert 'Bedeutung u. Begrundung des Glaubenssinnes (sensus fidei) als eines dogmatischen Erkenntniskriteriums' *Catholica* 25 (1971) 271-303 (bibliography); and, since this important study, J. M. R. Tillard 'A· propos du sensus fidelium' *Proche Orient Chrétien* 25 (1975) 113-134; L.M.F. de Troconiz y Sasigain *'Sensus fidei'; Logica connatural de la existencia cristiana. Un estudio del recurso al 'sensus fidei' en la teologia catolica de 1930 a 1970* (Vitoria 1976) (forthcoming publication of the first two parts); J. Sâncho Bielsa *Infalibilidad del pueblo do Dios. 'Sensus fidei' e infalibilidad organica de la Iglesia en la const. 'Lumen Gentium' del Concilio Vaticane II* (Pamplona 1979).

25. There is a large literature on this subject throughout the world. So far as France and the

present situation is concerned, we should like to mention just two issues of two journals: *Le Supplement* 133, May 1980 'La Régulation de la foi'; *Les Quatre Fleuves* 12, 1980 (Les Théologiens et l'Eglise').

26. See Matt. 28:19-20; John 17:20; Rom. 12:7; 15:16; 1 Cor. 12:5 and 8; 2 Tim. 4:5; Acts 4:29; 6:2-4.

27. See Rom. 12:7; 1 Cor. 12:28; Eph. 4:11; Acts 13:1. And see also *Didache* XI, 2; XIII, 2; *The Shepherd of Hermas* nos. 13, 1; 92, 4; 102, 2 (according to the enumeration of R. Joly); *Barnabas* 1, 8; 4, 9.

28. See Newman's letters to canon Walter, 17 June 1867; to Lord Blackford, 15 August 1870; to Miss Froude, 28 July 1875; and the letter to the Duke of Norfolk, Ch. IX, no. 11 29. Paul VI, 13 June 1977, to the bishops of Portugal. Compare John Paul II at Washington, 7 October 1979.

30. 'Officium principalissimum', as St Thomas puts it in 3a. Q. 67, 2 ad 1. St Augustine and St Leo often speak in the same sense. Similarly the Council of Trent is cited in the sources of the Codex, can. 1327, and by *Lumen Gentium* § 25.

31. AAS 42, 1950, 568; D. Sch. 3885.

32. See our *La Tradition et les traditions*. I. Essai historique (Paris 1960) pp. 257 ff.

33. K. Rahner *Das Dynamische in der Kirche* (Freiburg 1958) pp. 39-40.

34. We should again like to cite in this connection J.-L. Leuba *Vatican II, La Révélation divine* (Unam Sanctam 70 b) (Paris 1968) pp. 493 ff.; J. Witte in *Concilium* 117 (1976) (French ed.) 55-66; A. Dumas *Le Supplément* 133, May 1980, 216 ff.; B. Lohse 'Die Tragweite der Unfehlbarkeits- frage' *Stimmen der Zeit* (July 1980) 405-412, etc.

35. It is in this way that Richard Baumann was condemned by the Oberkirchenrat of Wurtemberg in 1958; and pastor Paul Schulz on 21 January 1979. And see H.-M. Müller 'Bindung und Freiheit kirchlicher Lehre' *Zeitschrift f. Theol, u. Kirche* 77 (1980) 479-501.

36. See J. Meyendorff *Concilium* 117 (1976) 49-54 (French ed.); Michel Evdokimov 'Théologien et théologien laic dans l'Eglise orthodoxe' *Les quatre Fleuves* 12 (1980) 29-42.

37. Our article in *Concilium* 77 (1972) 43-68.

38. Y. Congar 'Apostolicité de ministère et apostolicité de doctrine' *Volk Gottes*: Festgabe J. Hôfer (Freiburg 1967) pp. 84-111; rewritten in *Ministères et Communion ecclesiale* (Paris 1971) pp. 51-94. Ratzinger has a fine way of putting it: 'Die Nachfolge ist die Gestalt der Ueberlieferung, die Ueberlieferung ist der Gehalt der Nachfolge' ('The succession is the form of the tradition, the tradition is the content of the succession') in 'Primat, *Episkopat* und Successio apostolica' *Episkopat u. Primat* (1961) p. 49.

39. *Lumen Gentium* § 15; and see also *Unitatis redintegratio* § 3, § 4.

Georg Denzler

Bulletin: The discussion about Bernhard Hasler's publications on the First Vatican Council

THE FIRST VATICAN COUNCIL called by Pius IX passionately discussed the *infallibility of the pope* and on 18 July 1870, with two votes against, it became dogma. The opposition minority abstained from the vote.

Just in time for the centenary, the professor of theology at Tübingen, *Hans Küng*, reopened the debate on infallibility, which had never completely died down, with his book *Unfehlbar? Eine Anfrage.*[1] At the same time his Swiss compatriot *August B. Hasler* was working on a thesis, which he presented a few years later to the University of Munich as a historical dissertation and published under the title *Pius IX (1846-1878), die päpstliche Unfehlbarkeit und das I. Vatikanische Konzil. Dogmatisierung und Durchsetzung einer Ideologie.*[2] Küng himself wrote an important introduction to Hasler's monograph, *Wie der Papst unfehlbar wurde. Macht und Ohnmacht eines Dogmas.*[3] (How the pope became infallible. Power and impotence of a dogma.) In it Küng, the systematic theologian paid Hasler the historian (who had previously obtained a doctorate in theology at the Gregorian University in Rome) a glowing tribute:

> At last we have a Catholic historian who also takes seriously those who were defeated at the time, and their arguments, which have often been propounded since then. He discusses exhaustively both the position of the episcopal opponents of infallibility and also the most vehement defenders of it—which harmonising interpreters often find so embarrassing. He lets them speak without softening, toning them down or explaining them away. His understandable one-sidedness corrects and balances previous one-sided historical accounts also by the use of new sources.

Hasler can seldom have received such words of praise. Usually he has had to defend himself against critics who used weighty reflections, factual argument or merely ideological protest to express their disagreement. If we leave out those who are merely distinguished by their good prose or who have only scant knowledge of the subject, the real experts can be counted on ten fingers: Franz Xaver Bantle, Josef Blank, Victor

Conzemius, Piet Fransen, Werner Küppers, Giacomo Martina, S.J., Otto Hermann Pesch, Klaus Schatz, S.J., Peter Stockmeier and Manfred Weitlauf.[4]

1. GENERAL CRITICISMS

Most criticis blame Hasler for his violent reaction and aggressively polemical tone. But they generally agree with him about biased history writing and the practice of concealing the truth in archives, viz., the Vatican secret archives. Hardly a single expert denies that he has used a large number of previously inaccessible sources. However, most of them swiftly add that Hasler has used his considerable historical material in a biased way, selecting all the events and witnesses against infallibility and—according to Martina, who sees it as a major fault—omitted the necessary source criticism.

Hasler,[5] on the other hand, stresses that the weakness of many parts of the case for infallibility only became clear to him during the course of his studies. He did not approach the acts and documents which led to the dogma of infallibility as false or suspect *a priori*. His object was not to write a complete history of Vatican I or a biography of Pius IX. His aim was to give a fuller account of the sources for the origin, debate and promulgation of the doctrine of infallibility.

Conzemius, Hasler's fiercest opponent, criticises the *'systematic narrowing down' of the Council's procedure to the question of papal infallibility*. The exclusion of the sociological, political and theological points of view makes it more difficult or even impossible to understand adequately the thinking and processes that led up to the definition of the strongly contested doctrine. This observation should be taken seriously if it is not simply a way of covering up the fundamental theological problem:

> In spite of his methodological deficiency and his sometimes all too transparent bias, the book establishes facts correctly and raises questions for history and theology. The practice of the majority vote at the Council is well described, the differences between pope and curia stand out more clearly than in other accounts, Rome's questionable tactics of suppression of the minority of bishops in opposition are well presented on the whole, as the religious and mystical fanaticism of the cult of the pope and Pius IX's own view of his office, and its effects on the promulgation of the dogma. . . . We can certainly agree with Hasler that the case for infallibility contained ideological elements.

Like Küng, Hasler is accused of holding an immensely exaggerated concept of infallibility, which does not correspond to the vocabulary of the dogma. *Schatz* in particular, an equally resolute but fairer opponent, finds that Hasler is deficient in modern hermeneutics and knowledge of historical contingency. He denies the thesis, which is not new, that Church historians (as theologians!) are subject to dogmatic presuppositions in their research, as Hasler claims. He claims that:

> The Church of Vatican I cannot declare that papal infallibility is historically contained in scripture and tradition, in a modern critical sense. It can only supervise magisterially the present day expression of the Church's teaching which derives from the historical critical process, that is in particular, decide that in the spiritual and social context of the nineteenth century, the nature of the Church, as it appears in scripture and tradition, involves, or can involve, among other things, primacy and infallibility.

If there is a big discrepancy between a truth of faith and an historical fact, the decisive factor, according to Schatz, is not the literal meaning of a defined doctrine, but the *decision by the whole Church* (reception) as to whether an already proclaimed dogma is also a universally binding proposition of faith. This is one of the major problems of the book.

2. THE COUNCIL'S FREEDOM OR LACK OF FREEDOM

Hasler maintains that most of the bishops were put under physical, and especially, moral pressure when they were obliged to state their position on infallibility. Although the pope tolerated a certain amount of freedom, this was purely tactics. But an unfree Council produces invalid decrees.

Experts on the subject of the Council like Conzemius, Martina and Schatz reply that the Council did not have complete freedom but it had sufficient.

Besides Cardinal Manning (Westminster) and Bishop Senestrey (Regensburg) the 79-year-old Pope Pius IX, the portrayal of whose character wavers amazement and contempt, was the protagonist. (By the way I think that Hasler's suggestion that the Dominican Cardinal Guidi, a moderate opponent of infallibility, was the pope's natural son, might well be true.) The question of *the pope's health* is more serious because 'without a doubt the spiritual structure of a responsible personality is a most important problem for every society, including the Church' (*Stockmeier*). It is certain that Mastai-Ferretti suffered from epilepsy in his youth, it is uncertain whether he was later partly or completely cured of it. We cannot deny his lack of honesty, unhealthy mysticism, heedless despotism and mental disturbances. However 'the material that Hasler (still on the question of infallibility) collects on the personality structure of Pius IX exceeds what is known to a shocking degree' (*Weitlauf*). Pius IX was definitely a case for a psychiatrist. Hasler's quoting of damning testimonies from psychologists (Matussek, Pongratz) was in the justified attempt to understand the man as well as possible. Vinzenz Pallotti (1796-1850), one of the most successful counsellors in Rome at the time, fell to his knees when Pius IX was elected, saying: 'Let us pray, great trouble lies before the Church'.[6]

Pius IX's view of the infallible nature of the papal *magisterium* was made clear in the way in which he proclaimed the dogma of the immaculate conception of Mary (1854) and in other teachings. 'It was clear that the pope's conscious will to define doctrine was greater than before' (*Schatz*). I agree with Hasler that, *without Pius IX, the dogma of papal infallibility would not have been proclaimed*. Because the pope saw he was opposed by a considerable minority of hesitant or dissenting bishops, he had to use pressure. Hasler's 'reference to the moral pressure that the pope put on the materially dependent bishops also concerns at least some of the bishops. . . . The inequality of opportunity between the majority and the minority at the Council is corroborated by many facts' (*Schatz*).

3. ARGUMENTS FOR AND AGAINST INFALLIBILITY

Hasler brings together the arguments from scripture and tradition used by the Council fathers for and against infallibility and comes to the conclusion that the minority who opposed infallibility had the better arguments, whereas the majority employed inappropriate or weaker ones. As a warning example of the dogmatising supported by the majority, the Bishop of Rottenburg, Karl Josef von Hefle cited the 'case' of Pope Honorarius I (625-638) whom the Sixth Ecumenical Council (681) and Pope Leo II (682-683) condemned as a heretic because of his monothelite pronouncements about Jesus Christ. Hasler also used the question of Honorarius in his battery against infallibility, but was accused by *Stockmeier* of lacking historical sense, because later discoveries cannot act as a measure for earlier times.

However Stockmeier says that Hasler 'has presented the process of historical argumentation in its full range and worked on the event's inaccessibility'. Stockmeier also agrees with Hasler that 'it was indeed the majority who were uncritical in their use of history' and even indirectly used falsehoods. *Schatz*, on the other hand, does not think highly of Hasler's care in this area. He thinks it would have been more to the point to work out what function papal infallibility was to fulfil in the infallibilists' idea of the Church. However he agrees that there was nothing in the New Testament or in the tradition of the first thousand years to support the doctrine of infallibility.

On this fundamental point *Blank* says, 'Since the pioneering work of Anton Vögtle (1958) no reputable Catholic exegete can hold that the New Testament gives any clear support for the papal primacy and infallibility. The proof from scripture upon which the dogma was based at the time cannot be held valid today. The same is true of the proof from tradition from the fathers of the Church'.

Because of his historical-dynamic view of tradition, *Schatz* holds that it was legitimate that 'in the second millenium a particular line predominated which then as a logical consequence led, through the social and political and also theological situation, to a culmination in the declaration of papal infallibility at Vatican I, even though this culmination was an exaggeration'. This touches upon the subject of interpretation, which was as important in the so-called subjugation history of the time as it is in the 'conquest' of the dogma in modern theology.

4. INTERPRETATION AND RECEPTION OF THE DOGMA

Hasler is of the opinion that the dogma of infallibility can only be understood *papally*, i.e., for infallible definitions on matters of faith or morals, the pope does not need the express agreement of the Church, either beforehand or afterwards.

The phrase accepted at the last moment makes plain the necessity of a maximalist interpretation: dogmatic decisions of the pope are infallible 'of themselves, not because of the agreement of the Church' (*ex sese non autem ex consensu Ecclesiae*). The disputed 'ex sese' is usually seen as a formulation directed against the Gallicans. It was in fact *Bantle*, who disagrees with Hasler's theological interpretation, who gave him unexpected historical support by quoting the unambiguous statement on the Council in the writing of Martin, Bishop of Paderborn. According to Martin, the agreement of the bishops to an infallible pronouncement on a matter of faith by the pope does not need to be expressed either before or afterwards.[7]

Schatz and *Martina* take the view that the dogma of infallibility is *capable of being regarded* in such a way that a broad interpretation fits it as well as a narrow one. It is important that the explanation of the text at the time was in harmony with the whole tradition of the Church. However the Bible and the tradition of the first millenium display a synodal-collegial exercise of the *magisterium*.

Even if we accept that all the bishops gave their obedience freely to the dogma in the sense intended by the majority, there remains the question of the *agreement of the whole Church*, i.e., not only the bishops but also theologians and laity. And this is disregarding the question of how far the Council can be held to be a real ecumenical Council, since neither the Orthodox nor the Protestants were represented. Shortly before he set off for the Council, Kettler, Bishop of Mainz, tried to calm his flock with the thought that at the gathering in Rome, decisions would not be taken by majorities but by the agreement of the whole teaching authority of the Church. The reality of the situation proves without any doubt that the required 'consensus ecclesiae', the agreement of bishops, theologians and laity, was conspicuously lacking on the question of infallibility, both then and even more so today.

Theologians today consider that the history of the development of the dogma from 1870 onwards is of decisive importance. The process of its reception by the faithful is the final test in the historical explanation of the definition. The magic word 'reception'—Y. Congar even speaks of 're-reception'—not only repairs a possible lack of freedom in the Council but also determines the final horizon of understanding. Attempts at reinterpretation of the dogma are often reminiscent of *high wire acrobatics*. If it is allowed that *magisterium* and theology should continually reinterpret dogmatic definitions, without having to establish the statement of their historical core, and if they may take this interpretation to such a point that in the end the contrary to the previously intended and dogmatically defined meaning appears, then dogma as a formula of faith with an unchangeable historical core has completely lost its meaning. Moreover historians struggling for historical critical methods in theology would be completely wasting their time, because the church's *magisterium*, that is the pope as its highest representative, could decide quite independently which sense is authentic and to be believed.

5. DILEMMA BETWEEN HISTORY AND DOGMA

Bantle declares that the constantly quoted scripture passages (Matt. 16:18; Luke 22:32; John 22:15-17) and the tradition of the first millenium offer no proof of papal infallibility. This does not mean, as Hasler holds, that the doctrine of infallibility is unmasked as mere ideology. Because—and here Bantle performs a double *salto mortale*—even dogmatic formulations contain a 'surplus of meaning' that is only revealed after a long period of working out. This means in our case no more and no less than that we have only discovered after about a hundred years what the Council actually wanted to decree on infallibility: the narrowly defined sense supported by the opposition, who were defeated on the actual occasion. Thus the defeated of yesterday would become the winners of today.

Hasler's main concern was with a frequent contradiction between history and faith, particularly painfully in evidence in the dogma of the infallibility of the pope. In such conflicts he exposes and defines the historical expression of a doctrine but never forgets that dogma as an historical whole is subject to a continual *trial*. He is also aware of the danger that as a result of an overstretched view of reception, theologically based decisions are always determined by the *normativity of the factual*.

Otto H. Pesch reminds us: 'In the criticism made of Hasler up till now, there is no more painful argument than the frequently repeated statement that "we nowadays" do our work of theology with biblical and historical discoveries in quite a different way from the fathers of Vatican I and that since then, we in the Catholic Church have learned to think historically, so that we cannot hope, like Hasler, to determine the ways of thinking of Vatican I exactly'. *Knowledge of the historicity of dogma includes, in my view, admitting the possibility of error in definitions of faith.* And as soon as a mistaken definition is revealed as such, we should not try to get out of it by 'reinterpretation' but speak honestly of revising it. So it would be right to say today that when the infallibilists, with Pius IX as their leader, they ascribed absolute infallibility to the papal *magisterium*, i.e., in disconnecting the pope from the Bible and tradition and also the Church's sense of faith (*sensus fidelium*), they proclaimed a very historically determined view, which we are now slowly, although not completely, discarding in favour of a synodical and collegial primacy such as was practised in the early Church.

The thorny problem of the historicity of theological, even infallible theological teachings, is one of the most important for modern theology. *Weitlauf* rightly says: 'This side, the question of the historicity of the dogma of infallibility, as it was defined in 1870, has not yet found a satisfactory solution today. Let us hope that the initially furious reaction to Hasler's book will be followed by a rigorously factual study, concerned with the truth, on the broadest possible level.'

Translated by Dinah Livingstone

Notes

1. (Zurich/Einsiedeln/Cologne 1970.)
2. *Päpste und Papsttum* XII, ed. G. Denzler (Stuttgart 1977).
3. (Munich 1979, ²1980.) There are translations into Dutch, Spanish, English and Italian. After the Piper edition, there were editions from Ex Libris (Zurich 1981) and the paperback publisher Ullstein (Berlin 1981) which were enlarged by the addition of a bibliography about the case of Küng, a full list of the reviews of Hasler's work in the Piper edition (see note 2), the open letter of G. Denzler and A. B. Hasler to Pope John Paul II of 21 June 1980 and a postscript by G. Denzler. Only the dissertation edition (note 2) is suitable for scholarly discussion.
4. F. X. Bantle *Archivum Historiae Conciliorum II* (1979) pp. 182-219; J. Blank *Una Sancta* 33 (1978) pp. 72-82 and *Imprimatur* II (1978) pp. 56-59; V. Conzemius *Orientierung* 41 (1977) 207-209; P. Fransen *Theologie der Gegenwart* 22 (1979) pp. 43-49 and *Bijdragen* 39 (1978) pp. 447-456; W. Küppers *Kirche. Schweizerische Kirchenzeitung* 146 (1978) 190-194; G. Martina *L'Osservatore Romano*, 8 February 1978 and *Archivum Historiae Pontificiae* 16 (1978) pp. 341-369; O. H. Pesch *Deutches Allgemeines Sonntagsblatt* 11 March 1979 and 19 August 1979 and *Bilanz der Diskussion um die vatikanische Primatsund Unfehlbarkeitsdefinition: Papsttum als ökumenische Frage* (Munich-Mainz 1979) pp. 159-211; K. Schatz *Theologie und Philosophie* 53 (1978) pp. 248-276 and *La Civilta cattolica* 130 (1979) 245-258; P. Stockmeier *Münchener Theol. Zeitschrift* 29 (1978) 189-199; M. Weitlauf *Zeitschrift für Kirchengeschichte* 91 (1980) 94-105. For other reviews, see works mentioned in note 3.
5. Hasler was able to answer some criticisms in the Piper edition (see note 3). However, he died on 1 July 1980 when he was only 43 years old and can no longer defend himself. So I feel obliged to speak for my dead friend. I have followed the progress of his historical dissertation through many years and on many points I agree with him.
6. See *Ferment* 1 (1981) p. 25.
7. K. Martin *Der Wahre Sinn der vatikanische Lehrentscheidung über das unfehlbare päpstliche Lehramt* (Paderborn ²1871) pp. 18-19. Bishop Martin was a member of the Deputation on Faith at the Council. As a theologian he was supported by J. Kleutgen.

Contributors

BORIS BOBRINSKOY was born in Paris in 1925 and is married with three children. Since 1953 he has been professor of dogmatic theology at the St Sergius Institute of Orthodox Theology in Paris and since 1968 at the Institut Supérieur des Etudes Oecuméniques. From 1968 to 1979 he was rector of the French Orthodox parish of the Holy Trinity in Paris and since 1979 has been rector of the Russian Orthodox cathedral there. He is a member of the Faith and Order commission of the World Council of Churches. He has written numerous articles on the theology of the Trinity and the Eucharist and on the ecumenical movement.

LEONARDO BOFF was born in 1938 and is a Franciscan Friar. He is professor of dogmatic theology at the Philosophical-Theological Institute of Petrópolis (Rio de Janeiro), and theological adviser to the Bishop's conference of Brazil and the Conference of Brazilian and Latin American religious. He is the author of numerous books on Christology, liberation, the basic community, the faith in the Third World, etc., including *Jesus Christ, Liberator* (New York and London 1979).

YVES CONGAR, O.P., was born in Sedan, France, in 1904 and entered the Order of Preachers in 1925. He teaches at the Institut Superieur d'Etudes Oecumeniques of the Institut Catholique in Paris. His numerous publications include the following: *La Tradition et les traditions* (2 vols.) (1960 and 1963); *L'Ecclésiologie du haut moyen âge* (1963); *L'Eglise de St Augustin à l'époque moderne* (1970); *Une, sainte, catholique et apostolique* (1970); *Ministères et Communion écclesiale* (1971); *Un Peuple messianique. Salut et libération* (1976); *Eglise catholique et France moderne* (1978); *Je crois en l'Esprit Saint* (3 vols. (1979)).

GABRIEL DALY was born in Dublin in 1927, entered the Augustinian Order in 1944 and was ordained priest in 1951. He has degrees from the universities of the Gregorianum (Rome), Oxford and Hull. He teaches systematic theology at the Milltown Institute of Theology and Philosophy and the Irish School of Ecumenics. He has written *Transcendence and Immanence: A Study in Catholic Modernism and Integralism* (Oxford 1980) and has contributed chapters to *Irish Anglicanism* ed. M. Hurley (Dublin 1970); *Witness to the Spirit* ed. W. Harrington (Dublin 1979) and *Understanding Human Rights* ed. A. Falconer (Dublin 1980). He also contributes articles and reviews to *The Irish Theological Quarterly*, *The Heythrop Journal*, etc.

GEORG DENZLER was born in Bamberg in 1930. He studied philosophy and theology in Bamberg, continued his theological studies in Munich, obtained a doctorate there in 1962 and in 1967 was admitted to the faculty of Church History, having been ordained priest in 1955. Between 1963-69 he was theological assistant in Munich and also lecturer in Friesing from 1967-69. In 1969-70 he was visiting professor in Tübingen, and between 1970-71 lecturer in Munich University. Since 1971 he has been professor of church history at Bamberg. He was married in 1973 and has two children. His chief publications are *Kardinal Gugliemo Sirleto 1514-85* (Munich 1964); (with L. A. Dorn) *Tagebuch des Konzils* (Nürnberg/Eichstadt 1965); *Die Propagandakongregation in Rom und die Kirche in Deutschland im ersten Jahrzehnt nach dem Westfälischen Frieden* (Paderborn 1969); *Das Papsttum und der Amtszölibat* (2 vols.) (Stuttgart 1973-76); (with C. Andersen) *Wörterbuch der Kirchengeschichte* (Munich 1981). He has edited *Päpste und Papsttum* (18 volumes to date) (Stuttgart 1971 ff.); *Das Papsttum in der Diskussion* (Regensburg 1974); *Papsttum heute und morgen* (Regensburg 1975); *Kirche und Staat auf Distanz. Historische und aktuelle Perspektiven* (Munich 1977); *Priester für heute. Antworten auf das Schreiben Papst Johannes-Pauls II an die Priester* (Munich 1980); (with W. Gessel and J. Lehmann) *Bamberger Hochschulschriften*, 7 volumes (to date) (Bamberg 1979 ff.).

AVERY DULLES, S.J., has been a Jesuit since 1946, and a priest since 1956. He received his S.T.D. from the Gregorian University in 1960, and from then until 1974 taught theology at Woodstock College, both in Woodstock, Md. (1960-69) and in New York, N.Y. (1970-74). Since 1974 he has been professor of theology at the Catholic University of America. He has served as president (1975-76) of the Catholic Theological Society of America and as president (1978-79) of the American Theological Society. His publications include *Apologetics and the Biblical Christ* (Westminster 1963; London 1964); *Revelation Theology: A History* (New York 1969; London 1970); *A History of Apologetics* (London 1971; Philadelphia 1971); *The Survival of Dogma* (Garden City, N.Y. 1971); *Models of the Church* (Garden City, N.Y. 1974; Dublin 1976); *The Resilient Church* (Garden City, N.Y. 1977; Dublin 1978).

OLLE ENGSTRØM was born in 1920. He gained the degree of M.A. at Uppsala University in 1949, and was given an honorary doctorate at North Park College and Seminary, Chicago, USA in 1966. He has been dean of the Theological Seminary of the Mission Covenant Church of Sweden since 1962. He had earlier been General Secretary of the Free Church Council of Sweden and of the Free Church Christian Student Movement of Sweden, and was a member of the government committee on Church and State between 1958-68. Since 1978 he has been Moderator of Programme Unit III (Education and Renewal) of the World Council of Churches. He has been a member of the W.C.C. Central Committee since 1968.

BAS VAN IERSEL was born in 1924 at Heerlen in the Netherlands. He became a priest in 1950. He studied at the universities of Nijmegen and Louvain. He is a doctor of theology and is professor of New Testament exegesis at Nijmegen. He is also a member of the editorial board of the journals *Tijdschrift voor Theologie* and *Schrift*. One of his books is *'Der Sohn' in den synoptischen Jesusworten* (1961).

HARRY KUITERT was born in 1924 in Drachten (the Netherlands). After serving as a village vicar in the province of Zeeland he became university chaplain in Amsterdam and now teaches ethics and introductory dogmatic theology at the Free University of Amsterdam. Among his publications are *De mensvormigheid Gods* (1962); *The Reality of Faith* (1968); *Signals from the Bible* (1972); *Do you understand what you read?* (1970); *Zonder geloof vaart niemand wel* (1974); *Wat heet geloven?* (1977). His most recent publication on ethics is the article 'Ethik' in *Evangelisches Soziallexikon* (1980). He is the Protestant member of the editorial board of the *Tijdschrift voor Theologie*.

ULRICH KÜHN, born in 1932, studied (Protestant) theology at Leipzig, where he took his degree and gained his *Habilitation* in systematic theology. In 1964 he was ordained to the ministry of the Evangelical Lutheran Provincial Church of Saxony. He lectures in systematic and ecumenical theology at the (Protestant) Theological Institute in Leipzig. He is a member of the Faith and Order Commission of the World Council of Churches. His publications include: *Natur und Gnade. Untersuchungen zur deutschen katholischen Theologie der Gegenwart* (Berlin 1961); *Via caritatis. Theologie des Gesetzes bei Thomas von Aquin* (Berlin/Göttingen 1965); 'Das Abendmahl in der ökumenischen Theologie der Gegenwart' in *Theologische Realenzyklopädie* I (Berlin 1977) pp. 145-212; *Kirche* (*Handbuch Systematischer Theologie* 10) (Gütersloh 1980).

LUIGI SARTORI was born at Roana (Vicenza) in 1924 and studied at the Diocesan Seminary of Padua and the Gregorian University in Rome; he now teaches theology at Padua and Milan. He is the president of the Associazione Teologica Italiana, a member of 'Faith and Constitution' of the CEC (or COE). In addition to numerous articles and essays, he has also published *Blondel ed il Cristianesimo* (Padua 1953); *Teologia della storia* (Padua 1956); *E Dio il regista della storia?* (Milan 1961); *Spirito Santo e storia* (Rome 1979).

KURT STALDER was born in 1912 in the vicinity of Basle. He studied theology at the Old Catholic theological faculty of Berne University. (In Switzerland, incidentally, the official term for Old Catholic is *christkatholisch*, or literally 'Christian Catholic'.) He served as pastor of Grenchen, Solothurn, and in Berne. From 1960 on he has been professor of New Testament exegesis, homiletics and catechetics at the Old Catholic theological faculty in Berne. He is co-chairman of the official commission for Old Catholic/Roman Catholic dialogue in Switzerland and a member of other similar commissions. His publications include: *Das Werk des Geistes in der Heiligung bei Paulus* (Zürich 1962), and smaller studies covering such subjects as homiletics, catechetics, problems of historical research arising from the theory of knowledge and from methodological considerations, ecclesiology, canon law, and the relationship of language and extra-linguistic reality.

STEPHEN SYKES is the Van Mildert Professor of Divinity at the University of Durham. From 1964 to 1974 he was fellow and dean of St John's College, Cambridge, and university lecturer in divinity. He has written three books, *Friedrich Schleiermacher* (1971); *Christian Theology Today* (1971); *The Integrity of Anglicanism* (1979), (co-edited with J. P. Clayton) *Christ, Faith and History* (1972); and edited *Karl Barth, Studies of his Theological Method* (1980). In 1980 he published the first volume, co-edited with Derek Holmes, of *New Studies in Theology*.

CONCILIUM

1. (Vol. 1 No. 1) **Dogma.** Ed. Edward Schillebeeckx. 86pp.
2. (Vol. 2 No. 1) **Liturgy.** Ed. Johannes Wagner. 100pp.
3. (Vol. 3 No. 1) **Pastoral.** Ed. Karl Rahner. 104pp.
4. (Vol. 4 No. 1) **Ecumenism.** Hans Küng. 108pp.
5. (Vol. 5 No. 1) **Moral Theology.** Ed. Franz Bockle 98pp.
6. (Vol. 6 No. 1) **Church and World.** Ed. Johannes Baptist Metz. 92pp.
7. (Vol. 7 No. 1) **Church History.** Roger Aubert. 92pp.
8. (Vol. 8 No. 1) **Canon Law.** Ed. Teodoro Jimenez Urresti and Neophytos Edelby. 96pp.
9. (Vol. 9 No. 1) **Spirituality.** Ed. Christian Duquoc. 88pp.
10. (Vol. 10 No. 1) **Scripture.** Ed. Pierre Benoit and Roland Murphy. 92pp.
11. (Vol. 1 No. 2) **Dogma.** Ed. Edward Schillebeeckx. 88pp.
12. (Vol. 2 No. 2) **Liturgy.** Ed. Johannes Wagner. 88pp.
13. (Vol. 3 No. 2) **Pastoral.** Ed. Karl Rahner. 84pp.
14. (Vol. 4 No. 2) **Ecumenism.** Ed. Hans Küng. 96pp.
15. (Vol. 5 No. 2) **Moral Theology.** Ed. Franz Bockle. 88pp.
16. (Vol. 6 No. 2) **Church and World.** Ed. Johannes Baptist Metz. 84.pp.
17. (Vol. 7 No. 2) **Church History.** Ed. Roger Aubert. 96pp.
18. (Vol. 8 No. 2) **Religious Freedom.** Ed. Neophytos Edelby and Teodoro Jimenez Urresti. 96pp.
19. (Vol. 9 No. 2) **Religionless Christianity?** Ed. Christian Duquoc. 96pp.
20. (Vol. 10 No. 2) **The Bible and Tradition.** Ed. Pierre Benoit and Roland E. Murphy. 96pp.
21. (Vol. 1 No 3) **Revelation and Dogma.** Ed. Edward Schillebeeckx. 88pp.
22. (Vol. 2 No. 3) **Adult Baptism and Initiation.** Ed. Johannes Wagner. 96pp.
23. (Vol. 3 No. 3) **Atheism and Indifference.** Ed. Karl Rahner. 92pp.
24. (Vol. 4 No. 3) **The Debate on the Sacraments.** Ed. Hans Küng. 92pp.
25. (Vol. 5 No. 3) **Morality, Progress and History.** Ed. Franz Bockle. 84pp.
26. (Vol. 6 No. 3) **Evolution.** Ed. Johannes Baptist Metz. 88pp.
27. (Vol. 7 No. 3) **Church History.** Ed. Roger Aubert. 92pp.
28. (Vol. 8 No. 3) **Canon Law—Theology and Renewal.** Ed. Neophytos Edelby and Teodoro Jimenez Urresti. 92pp.
29. (Vol. 9 No. 3) **Spirituality and Politics.** Ed. Christian Duquoc. 84pp.
30. (Vol. 10 No. 3) **The Value of the Old Testament.** Ed. Pierre Benoit and Roland Murphy. 92pp.
31. (Vol. 1 No. 4) **Man, World and Sacrament.** Ed. Edward Schillebeeckx. 84pp.
32. (Vol. 2 No. 4) **Death and Burial: Theology and Liturgy.** Ed. Johannes Wagner. 88pp.

33. (Vol. 3 No. 4) **Preaching the Word of God.** Ed. Karl Rahner. 96pp.
34. (Vol. 4 No. 4) **Apostolic by Succession?** Ed. Hans Küng. 96pp.
35. (Vol. 5 No. 4) **The Church and Social Morality.** Ed. Franz Bockle. 92pp.
36. (Vol. 6 No. 4) **Faith and the World of Politics.** Ed. Johannes Baptist Metz 96pp.
37. (Vol. 7 No. 4) **Prophecy.** Ed. Roger Aubert. 80pp.
38. (Vol. 8 No. 4) **Order and the Sacraments.** Ed. Neophytos Edelby and Teodoro Jimenez Urresti. 96pp.
39. (Vol. 9 No. 4) **Christian Life and Eschatology.** Ed. Christian Duquoc. 94pp.
40. (Vol. 10 No. 4) **The Eucharist: Celebrating the Presence of the Lord.** Ed. Pierre Benoit and Roland Murphy. 88pp.
41. (Vol. 1 No. 5) **Dogma.** Ed. Edward Schillebeeckx. 84pp.
42. (Vol. 2 No. 5) **The Future of the Liturgy.** Ed. Johannes Wagner. 92pp.
43. (Vol. 3 No. 5) **The Ministry and Life of Priests Today.** Ed. Karl Rahner. 104pp.
44. (Vol. 4 No. 5) **Courage Needed.** Ed. Hans Küng. 92pp.
45. (Vol. 5 No. 5) **Profession and Responsibility in Society.** Ed. Franz Bockle. 84pp.
46. (Vol. 6 No. 5) **Fundamental Theology.** Ed. Johannes Baptist Metz. 84pp.
47. (Vol. 7 No. 5) **Sacralization in the History of the Church.** Ed. Roger Aubert. 80pp.
48. (Vol. 8 No. 5) **The Dynamism of Canon Law.** Ed. Neophytos Edelby and Teodoro Jimenez Urresti. 92pp.
49. (Vol. 9 No. 5) **An Anxious Society Looks to the Gospel.** Ed. Christian Duquoc. 80pp.
50. (Vol. 10 No. 5) **The Presence and Absence of God.** Ed. Pierre Benoit and Roland Murphy. 88pp.
51. (Vol. 1 No. 6) **Tension between Church and Faith.** Ed. Edward Schillebeeckx. 160pp.
52. (Vol. 2 No. 6) **Prayer and Community.** Ed. Herman Schmidt. 156pp.
53. (Vol. 3 No. 6) **Catechetics for the Future.** Ed. Alois Müller. 168pp.
54. (Vol. 4 No. 6) **Post-Ecumenical Christianity.** Ed. Hans Küng. 168pp.
55. (Vol. 5 No. 6) **The Future of Marriage as Institution.** Ed. Franz Bockle. 180pp.
56. (Vol. 6 No. 6) **Moral Evil Under Challenge.** Ed. Johannes Baptist Metz. 160pp.
57. (Vol. 7 No. 6) **Church History at a Turning Point.** Ed. Roger Aubert. 160pp.
58. (Vol. 8 No. 6) **Structures of the Church's Presence in the World of Today.** Ed. Teodoro Jimenez Urresti. 160pp.
59. (Vol. 9 No. 6) **Hope.** Ed. Christian Duquoc. 160pp.
60. (Vol. 10 No. 6) **Immortality and Resurrection.** Ed. Pierre Benoit

and Roland Murphy. 160pp.
61. (Vol. 1 No. 7) **The Sacramental Administration of Reconciliation.** Ed. Edward Schillebeeckx. 160pp.
62. (Vol. 2 No. 7) **Worship of Christian Man Today.** Ed. Herman Schmidt. 156pp.
63. (Vol. 3 No. 7) **Democratization of the Church.** Ed. Alois Müller. 160pp.
64. (Vol. 4 No. 7) **The Petrine Ministry in the Church.** Ed. Hans Küng. 160pp.
65. (Vol. 5 No. 7) **The Manipulation of Man.** Ed. Franz Bockle. 144pp.
66. (Vol. 6 No. 7) **Fundamental Theology in the Church.** Ed. Johannes Baptist Metz. 156pp.
67. (Vol. 7 No. 7) **The Self-Understanding of the Church.** Ed. Roger Aubert. 144pp.
68. (Vol. 8 No. 7) **Contestation in the Church.** Ed. Teodoro Jimenez Urresti. 152pp.
69. (Vol. 9 No. 7) **Spirituality, Public or Private?** Ed. Christian Duquoc. 156pp.
70. (Vol. 10 No. 7) **Theology, Exegesis and Proclamation.** Ed. Roland Murphy. 160pp.
71. (Vol. 1 No. 8) **The Bishop and the Unity of the Church.** Ed. Edward Schillebeeckx. 156pp.
72. (Vol. 2 No. 8) **Liturgy and the Ministry.** Ed. Herman Schmidt. 160pp.
73. (Vol. 3 No. 8) **Reform of the Church.** Ed. Alois Müller and Norbert Greinacher. 152pp.
74. (Vol. 4 No. 8) **Mutual Recognition of Ecclesial Ministries?** Ed. Hans Küng and Walter Kasper. 152pp.
75. (Vol. 5 No. 8) **Man in a New Society.** Ed. Franz Bockle. 160pp.
76. (Vol. 6 No. 8) **The God Question.** Ed. Johannes Baptist Metz. 156pp.
77. (Vol. 7 No. 8) **Election-Consensus-Reception.** Ed. Giuseppe Alberigo and Anton Weiler. 156pp.
78. (Vol. 8 No. 8) **Celibacy of the Catholic Priest.** Ed. William Bassett and Peter Huizing. 160pp.
79. (Vol. 9 No. 8) **Prayer.** Ed. Christian Duquoc and Claude Geffré. 126pp.
80. (Vol. 10 No. 8) **Ministries in the Church.** Ed. Bas van Iersel and Roland Murphy. 152pp.
81. **The Persistence of Religion.** Ed. Andrew Greeley and Gregory Baum. 0 8164 2537 X 168pp.
82. **Liturgical Experience of Faith.** Ed. Herman Schmidt and David Power. 0 8164 2538 8 144pp.
83. **Truth and Certainty.** Ed. Edward Schillebeeckx and Bas van Iersel. 0 8164 2539 6 144pp.
84. **Political Commitment and Christian Community.** Ed. Alois Müller and Norbert Greinacher. 0 8164 2540 X 156pp.
85. **The Crisis of Religious Language** Ed. Johannes Baptist Metz and Jean-Pierre Jossua. ,0 8164 2541 8 144pp.
86. **Humanism and Christianity.** Ed.

Claude Geffré. 0 8164 2542 6 144pp.
87. **The Future of Christian Marriage.** Ed. William Bassett and Peter Huizing. 0 8164 2575 2.
88. **Polarization in the Church.** Ed. Hans Küng and Walter Kasper. 0 8164 2572 8 156pp.
89. **Spiritual Revivals.** Ed. Christian Duquoc and Casiano Floristán. 0 8164 2573 6 156pp.
90. **Power and the Word of God.** Ed. Franz Bockle and Jacques Marie Pohier. 0 8164 2574 4 156pp.
91. **The Church as Institution.** Ed. Gregory Baum and Andrew Greeley. 0 8164 2575 2 168pp.
92. **Politics and Liturgy.** Ed. Herman Schmidt and David Power. 0 8164 2576 0 156pp.
93. **Jesus Christ and Human Freedom.** Ed. Edward Schillebeeckx and Bas van Iersel. 0 8164 2577 9 168pp.
94. **The Experience of Dying.** Ed. Norbert Greinacher and Alois Müller. 0 8164 2578 7 156pp.
95. **Theology of Joy.** Ed. Johannes Baptist Metz and Jean-Pierre Jossua. 0 8164 2579 5 164pp.
96. **The Mystical and Political Dimension of the Christian Faith.** Ed. Claude Geffré and Gustavo Guttierez. 0 8164 2580 9 168pp.
97. **The Future of the Religious Life.** Ed. Peter Huizing and William Bassett. 0 8164 2094 7 96pp.
98. **Christians and Jews.** Ed. Hans Küng and Walter Kasper. 0 8164 2095 5 96pp.
99. **Experience of the Spirit.** Ed. Peter Huizing and William Bassett. 0 8164 2096 3 144pp.
100. **Sexuality in Contemporary Catholicism.** Ed. Franz Bockle and Jacques Marie Pohier. 0 8164 2097 1 126pp.
101. **Ethnicity.** Ed. Andrew Greeley and Gregory Baum. 0 8164 2145 5 120pp.
102. **Liturgy and Cultural Religious Traditions.** Ed. Herman Schmidt and David Power. 0 8164 2146 2 120pp.
103. **A Personal God?** Ed. Edward Schillebeeckx and Bas van Iersel. 0 8164 2149 8 142pp.
104. **The Poor and the Church.** Ed. Norbert Greinacher and Alois Müller. 0 8164 2147 1 128pp.
105. **Christianity and Socialism.** Ed. Johannes Baptist Metz and Jean-Pierre Jossua. 0 8164 2148 X 144pp.
106. **The Churches of Africa: Future Prospects.** Ed. Claude Geffré and Bertrand Luneau. 0 8164 2150 1 128pp.
107. **Judgement in the Church.** Ed. William Bassett and Peter Huizing. 0 8164 2166 8 128pp.
108. **Why Did God Make Me?** Ed. Hans Küng and Jürgen Moltmann. 0 8164 2167 6 112pp.

109. **Charisms in the Church.** Ed. Christian Duquoc and Casiano Floristán. 0 8164 2168 4 128pp.
110. **Moral Formation and Christianity.** Ed. Franz Bockle and Jacques Marie Pohier. 0 8164 2169 2 120pp.
111. **Communication in the Church.** Ed. Gregory Baum and Andrew Greeley. 0 8164 2170 6 126pp.
112. **Liturgy and Human Passage.** Ed. David Power and Luis Maldonado. 0 8164 2608 2 136pp.
113. **Revelation and Experience.** Ed. Edward Schillebeeckx and Bas van Iersel. 0 8164 2609 0 134pp.
114. **Evangelization in the World Today.** Ed. Norbert Greinacher and Alois Müller. 0 8164 2610 4 136pp.
115. **Doing Theology in New Places.** Ed. Jean-Pierre Jossua and Johannes Baptist Metz. 0 8164 2611 2 120pp.
116. **Buddhism and Christianity.** Ed. Claude Geffré and Mariasusai Dhavamony. 0 8164 2612 0 136pp.
117. **The Finances of the Church.** Ed. William Bassett and Peter Huizing. 0 8164 2197 8 160pp.
118. **An Ecumenical Confession of Faith?** Ed. Hans Küng and Jürgen Moltmann. 0 8164 2198 6 136pp.
119. **Discernment of the Spirit and of Spirits.** Ed. Casiano Floristán and Christian Duquoc. 0 8164 2199 4 136pp.
120. **The Death Penalty and Torture.** Ed. Franz Bockle and Jacques Marie Pohier. 0 8164 2200 1 136pp.
121. **The Family in Crisis or in Transition.** Ed. Andrew Greely. 0 567 30001 3 128pp.
122. **Structures of Initiation in Crisis.** Ed. Luis Maldonado and David Power. 0 567 30002 1 128pp.
123. **Heaven.** Ed. Bas van Iersel and Edward Schillebeeckx. 0 567 30003 X 120pp.
124. **The Church and the Rights of Man.** Ed. Alois Müller and Norbert Greinacher. 0 567 30004 8 140pp.
125. **Christianity and the Bourgeoisie.** Ed. Johannes Baptist Metz. 0 567 30005 6 144pp.
126. **China as a Challenge to the Church.** Ed. Claude Geffré and Joseph Spae. 0 567 30006 4 136pp.
127. **The Roman Curia and the Communion of Churches.** Ed. Peter Huizing and Knut Walf. 0 567 30007 2 144pp.
128. **Conflicts about the Holy Spirit.** Ed. Hans Küng and Jürgen Moltmann. 0 567 30008 0 144pp.
129. **Models of Holiness.** Ed. Christian Duquoc and Casiano Floristán. 0 567 30009 9 128pp.
130. **The Dignity of the Despised of the Earth.** Ed. Jacques Marie

Pohier and Dietmar Mieth. 0 567 30010 2 144pp.
131. **Work and Religion.** Ed. Gregory Baum. 0 567 30011 0 148pp.
132. **Symbol and Art in Worship.** Ed. Luis Maldonado and David Power. 0 567 30012 9 136pp.
133. **Right of the Community to a Priest.** Ed. Edward Schillebeeckx and Johannes Baptist Metz. 0 567 30013 7 148pp.
134. **Women in a Men's Church.** Ed. Virgil Elizondo and Norbert Greinacher. 0 567 30014 5 144pp.
135. **True and False Universality of Christianity.** Ed. Claude Geffré and Jean-Pierre Jossua. 0 567 30015 3 138pp.
136. **What is Religion? An Inquiry for Christian Theology.** Ed. Mircea Eliade and David Tracy. 0 567 30016 1 98pp.
137. **Electing our Own Bishops.** Ed. Peter Huizing and Knut Walf. 0 567 30017 X 112pp.
138. **Conflicting Ways of Interpreting the Bible.** Ed. Hans Küng and Jürgen Moltmann. 0 567 30018 8 112pp.
139. **Christian Obedience.** Ed. Casiano Floristán and Christian Duquoc. 0 567 30019 6 96pp.
140. **Christian Ethics and Economics: the North-South Conflict.** Ed. Dietmar Mieth and Jacques Marie Pohier. 0 567 30020 X 128pp.

1981
141. **Neo-Conservatism: Social and Religious Phenomenon.** Ed. Gregory Baum and John Coleman. 0 567 30021 8.
142. **The Times of Celebration.** Ed. David Power and Mary Collins. 0 567 30022 6.
143. **God and Father.** Ed. Edward Schillebeeckx and Johannes Baptist Metz. 0 567 30023 4.
144. **Tensions Between the Churches of the First World and the Third World.** Ed. Virgil Elizondo and Norbert Greinacher. 0 567 30024 2.
145. **Nietzsche and Christianity.** Ed. Claude Geffré and Jean-Pierre Jossua. 0 567 30025 0.
146. **Where Does the Church Stand?** Ed. Giuseppe Alberigo. 0 567 30026 9.
147. **The Revised Code of Canon Law: a Missed Opportunity?** Ed. Peter Huizing and Knut Walf. 0 567 30027 7.
148. **Who Has the Say in the Church?** Ed. Hans Küng and Jürgen Moltmann. 0 567 30028 5.
149. **Francis of Assisi: an Example?** Ed. Casiano Floristán and Christian Duquoc. 0 567 30029 3.
150. **One Faith, One Church, Many Moralities?** Ed. Jacques Pohier and Dietmar Mieth. 0 567 30030 7.

All back issues are still in print and available for sale. Orders should be sent to the publishers,

T. & T. CLARK LIMITED
36 George Street, Edinburgh EH2 2LQ, Scotland